COMPASS

A GUIDEBOOK TO ENGLISH GRAMMAR

SECOND EDITION, REVISED

Roumpini Papadomichelaki, J.D., M.A., MEd

Lash Keith Vance, Ph.D., M.A., MEd

The Write Press, Inc

[Handwritten annotations:]

Conjunction: Used to connect clauses

Conjunctive adverb - show cause and effect, sequence to coordinate ideas or contrast, comparison or other relationships

adverb: relating 2 time, circumstance, manner, cause, degree (gently, quite, then, there)

preposition: ex. the man on the platform / she arrived after dinner

The Write Press, Inc

COMPASS
A Guidebook to English Grammar
Second Edition—Revised

Photos provided by The Write Press and istockphotos.com.

ISBN-13: 978-0-9820005-1-9
ISBN-10: 0-9820005-1-0

TABLE OF CONTENTS

CHAPTER 1: PARTS OF SPEECH 1

Nouns 2
Noun Definitions...2
Noun Characteristics..3
Noun 3
Number 3
Noun 3
Case 3
Noun Number and Case 4
Noun Types 7
Common Nouns..7
Proper Nouns 7
Count Nouns...8
Non-Count Nouns..8

Pronouns 12
Pronoun Definitions..12
Pronoun Characteristics...13
Pronoun...13
Number 13
Pronoun Gender..13
Pronoun Person...13
Pronoun Case 13
Pronoun Types...13
Personal Pronouns..14
Intensive Pronouns...15
Reflexive Pronouns...15
Relative Pronouns..16
Interrogative Pronouns..17
Demonstrative Pronouns..17
Reciprocal Pronouns...18
Indefinite Pronouns..19

Adjectives 22
Adjective Definitions 22
Adjective Characteristics: 24
Degrees of Intensity 24
Adjective Types...26
Descriptive (Modifying)..26
Specifying (Limiting)..26

Verbs 30
Verb Definitions..30
Verb Characteristics:...32
Verb 32

Person 32

Verb Number 32

Verb Tense 32

Verb Mood 32

Verb Voice 32

Verb Types 33

Main Verbs 33

Auxiliary (Helping) Verbs 33

Linking Verbs 34

Transitive Verbs 34

Intransitive Verbs 35

The Base Form 36

Verb Forms 36

The Simple Present Tense Form: (–s Form) 36

The Simple Past Tense Form: (–ed Form) 36

The Past Participle Form: (–ed Form) 37

The Present Participle Form: (–ing Form) 37

The Infinitive Form: (to- Form) 38

Adverbs 42

Adverb Definitions 42

Adverb Types 44

Descriptive Adverbs 44

Conjunctive (Descriptive) Adverbs 45

Relative Adverbs 46

Conjunctions 50

Conjunction Definitions 50

Conjunction Types 52

Coordinating Conjunctions 52

Subordinating Conjunctions 52

Correlative Conjunctions 53

Prepositions 57

Preposition Definitions 57

Preposition as Adjective 59

Preposition as Adverb 59

Preposition as Part of Phrasal Verb 59

PREPOSITION TYPES 59

Interjections 64

Interjection Definitions 64

CHAPTER 2: VERB TENSES 67

VERB TENSES 68

Verb Tense Definitions 68

Time Dimensions 69

Time Circumstances 69

Simple Tenses 71

Repetition/ (Completion) 71
Perfect Progressive Tenses 72
Continuation/Duration 72

Present tenses 75
Simple Present Tense...75
Present Progressive Tense 76
Present Perfect Tense 77
Present Perfect Progressive Tense 77

Past Tenses 81
Simple Past Tense 81
Past Progressive Tense 82
Past Perfect Tense..82
Past Perfect Progressive Tense 83

Future Tenses 86
Simple Future Tense 86
Future Progressive Tense 86
Future Perfect Tense 87
Future Perfect Progressive Tense 87

Verb Tense Charts 86
Present Tense Chart...90
Past Tense Chart 91
Future Tense Chart 92
Irregular Verb Chart 93
Most Common Auxilliary Verbs: 94

CHAPTER 3: SENTENCE STRUCTURES 97

Phrases 99

Phrase Definitions 99
Phrase Types 100
Noun Phrases 100
Verb Phrases...100
Participial Phrases 101
Infinitive Phrases 101
Prepositional Phrases 102
Absolute Phrases 103

Clauses 106

Clause Definitions...106
Clause Characteristics 107
Simple Subject 107
Compound Subject 107
Complete Subject 108
Simple Predicate 109
Compound Predicate 109
Complete Predicate 110
Clause Types 115
Independent Clause 115
Dependent Clause 115
Adverb (Dependent) Clause 116
Adjective (Dependent) Clause 116

Noun (Dependent) Clause 117

Words of Dependence 120
RELATIVE PRONOUNS 120
RELATIVE ADVERBS 120
SUBORDINATING CONJUNCTIONS 121

Sentences 123

Sentence Definitions 123
Sentence Purposes 124
Declarative Sentences 124
Interrogative Sentences 124
Imperative Sentences 124
Exclamatory Sentences 124
Sentence Types 125
Simple Sentences 125
Compound Sentences 127
Complex Sentences 128
Compound-Complex Sentences 129

CHAPTER 4: AGREEMENT 135

SUBJECT/VERB AGREEMENT: 136
FOUR IMPORTANT STEPS 136
STEP 1: Find the verb(s) of your clause 136
STEP 2: Find the subject(s) of your clause 136
STEP 3: Make sure that the verb and its subject agree in number 137
STEP 4: Make sure that the verb and its pronoun subject agree in person (1st, 2nd, 3rd) 137
Agreement Rules: Subjects 138
NUMBER / PERSON 138
SUBJECT/VERB ORDER 138
COMPOUND SUBJECT 139
SUBJECT WITH CONJUNCTIONS OTHER THAN "AND" 139
SUBJECT WITH MODIFIERS 139
SUBJECT vs. SUBJECT COMPLEMENT 140
SUBJECT/VERB AGREEMENT: NOUNS AS SUBJECTS 140
NON-COUNT NOUNS AS SUBJECTS 140
COLLECTIVE NOUNS AS SUBJECTS 141
SPECIAL NOUNS AS SUBJECTS 142
SUBJECT/VERB AGREEMENT: PRONOUNS AS SUBJECTS 143
RELATIVE PRONOUNS AS SUBJECTS 143
INDEFINITE PRONOUNS AS SUBJECTS 143

PRONOUN/ANTECEDENT AGREEMENT: 144
Six important steps 144
STEP 1: Find the pronoun(s) 144
STEP 2: Find the antecedent of your pronoun 145
STEP 3: Make sure that the pronoun and its antecedent agree in number (singular or plural) 146
STEP 4: Make sure that the pronoun and its antecedent agree in person (1st, 2nd, 3rd) 146
STEP 5: Make sure that the pronoun and its antecedent agree in gender (female, male, neuter) 147
STEP 6: Make sure to avoid sexist language 147
Agreement Rules: Pronouns 148
COMPOUND ANTECEDENT 148

ANTECEDENT WITH CONJUNCTIONS OTHER THAN "AND" 148
PRONOUN/ANTECEDENT AGREEMENT: 149
NOUNS AS ANTECEDENTS 149
NON-COUNT NOUNS AS ANTECEDENTS..149
COLLECTIVE NOUNS AS ANTECEDENTS 149
PRONOUN/ANTECEDENT AGREEMENT: 150
PRONOUNS AS ANTECEDENTS..150
INDEFINITE PRONOUNS AS ANTECEDENTS 150

CHAPTER 5: SENTENCE ERRORS **151**

FRAGMENTS...**152**
Fragment Basics..152
FRAGMENT DEFINITION 152
FRAGMENT IDENTIFICATION 153
FRAGMENT CORRECTION 154

Run On & Comma Splice...**157**
Run-On & Comma-Splice Basics 157
RUN-ON & COMMA-SPLICE DEFINITIONS 157
RUN-ON & COMMA-SPLICE IDENTIFICATION 158
RUN-ON & COMMA-SPLICE CORRECTION 160

MIXED CONSTRUCTION **162**
Mixed-Construction Basics 162
MIXED-CONSTRUCTION DEFINITION 162
MIXED-CONSTRUCTION IDENTIFICATION 163
MIXED-CONSTRUCTION CORRECTION 164

MISPLACED MODIFIER..**166**
Misplaced-Modifier Basics 166
MISPLACED-MODIFIER DEFINITION...166
MISPLACED-MODIFIER IDENTIFICATION & CORRECTION 167

DANGLING MODIFIER...**169**
Dangling-Modifier Basics 169
DANGLING-MODIFIER DEFINITION..169
DANGLING-MODIFIER IDENTIFICATION & CORRECTION 170

APPENDIX for CHAPTER 1: PARTS OF SPEECH...**173**

APPENDIX for CHAPTER 2: VERB TENSES..**204**

APPENDIX for CHAPTER 3: SENTENCE STRUCTURES **215**

APPENDIX for CHAPTER 4: AGREEMENT **226**

APPENDIX for CHAPTER 5: SENTENCE ERRORS..**237**

Chapter 1
Parts of Speech

Parts of speech are the building blocks of language. In English, there are eight distinct categories of such building blocks: **Nouns, Pronouns, Adjectives, Verbs, Adverbs, Conjunctions, Prepositions, and Interjections**. To construct language correctly, one needs to be familiar with both the form and the function of these building blocks as well as to follow certain rules about their usage; otherwise, if one uses these building blocks incorrectly, then the overall structure will suffer.

NOUNS

NOUN DEFINITIONS

Formal Definition

Form: Nouns are the words used to identify and name persons, places, things, and ideas. Their form as singular or plural conveys information about their quantity or number while their position in the sentence often conveys information about their function.

Function: In a sentence, nouns can function in many different ways. Nouns can be subjects, objects, complements, and modifiers. Their specific function within the sentence determines the *case* of the noun (subjective, objective, possessive/ modifier).

Etymology: The word *noun* derives from the Latin word *nomen*, meaning *name*. This is exactly what nouns do: they name persons, places, things, and ideas.

Informal Definition

*Imagine you are the director of a movie or a play. You walk onto the scene, and nothing is there. You realize immediately that you need to decide on four distinct and fundamental elements of your movie or play: the **actors** (persons), the **setting** (places), the **props** (things), and the **message** (ideas). Without these things, you cannot produce a movie or even a commercial.*

Person	Place	Thing	Idea

Westminster Guard	Yosemite	Spider	Desolation

Travelogue

June 10th, 2006

Greece, Crete, The Bakery

Have you ever traveled to a foreign country (place) and felt frustrated by not being able to communicate? Well, I have. This morning (idea-time) I set off in pursuit (idea) of breakfast (thing). My budget (thing) forced me to stay away from restaurants (place) and experiment with local bakeries (place). One problem (idea), however, is that in Greece many bakeries (place), unlike restaurants (place), don't have a menu (thing) in English (idea), so I had to rely on sign language (idea). I entered the small bakery (place) that had loaves (thing) of bread (thing) and syrupy desserts (thing) on nearly every shelf (thing). Some even were baked in the shape (idea) of chickens (thing)! Not wanting a dessert (thing), I pointed to a loaf (thing) of bread (thing), and the sales assistant (person) responded, "thelete to psomi?" Well, of course her speech (idea) sounded entirely Greek to me. However, she was quite compassionate for this ignorant tourist (person), and handing the loaf (thing) to me she repeated the word (thing), "psomi". I repeated after her and smiled for having learned my first Greek noun (thing), "psomi," the Greek word (thing) that names bread (thing). Knowing nouns (thing) can at least get you fed!

NOUN CHARACTERISTICS

Noun Number

Depending on their form, nouns convey information about the number of persons, places, things, or ideas. With most regular nouns, the plural is formed by adding an "s" at the end of the noun. This indicates more than one person, place, thing, or idea in number. For example, these words form the plural by adding an "s": student(s), professor(s), desk(s), etc. However, English does have a number of exceptions and irregular nouns. If you are unsure, you should consult a dictionary for correct usage.

Noun Case

Nouns convey information about their function as subjects (subjective case), objects (objective case), complements (subjective or objective case), or possessives/modifiers (possessive case); typically this depends on their position in the sentence (subjects typically precede verbs) although this is not without exceptions. Their form only changes in the possessive case.

Noun Number and Case

Number	Subjective Case noun=subject	Objective Case noun=object	Possessive Case noun=possession
Singular	The **student** lost his book.	The professor lent the **student** a book.	The **student's** book was found.
Plural	The **students** lost their books.	The professor lent the **students** books.	The **students'** books were found.

Highlight Points:

Possessive Case

A. Singular Nouns

- That end with an –s:

Add an apostrophe and–s **OR** an apostrophe

> *A **compass's** (or **compass'**) purpose is guidance*

- That do not end with an –s:

Add and apostrophe and an –s

> *The **student's** book was found.*

C. More than one Noun

- That share possession:

Add an apostrophe to the last noun.

> *Mary and **John's** novels (they are co-authors of the same novels).*

- That have individual possession:

> *Mary's and **John's** novels (Mary is the author of one or more novels, and John of others; they are not co-authors of the same ones.)*

B. Plural Nouns

- That end with an –s (regular):

Add and apostrophe

> *The **students'** books were found.*

- That do not end with an –s (irregular):

Add an apostrophe and an –s

> *The **women's** basketball team won the game.*

D. Alternative Possession

- A prepositional phrase with "of":

> *The **student's** book was found. OR*
> *The **book of the student** was found.*

Preferably use the apostrophe rules for persons and animals. For other nouns use the "of" phrase possession.

NOUN NUMBER BASICS

Nouns change their form to convey information about the number (one or more) of persons, places, things, or ideas. Most nouns form the plural by adding an "s" or "es" at the end. However, English has a number of exceptions and irregular plurals. The following are some of the categories and exceptions, but you can always consult a dictionary in case you are unsure.

Regular Nouns:
Add –s at the end.

instructor	*instructors*
classroom	*classrooms*
course	*courses*

Regular Nouns ending in ch, s, sh, x, z: Add –es at the end.

coach	*coaches*
class	*classes*
dash	*dashes*
box	*boxes*
quiz	*quizzes*

Nouns ending in o:
Add either –s or –es.

piano	*pianos*
ghetto	*ghettos*
photo	*photos*
studio	*studios*
video	*videos*
tomato	*tomatoes*
echo	*echoes*

Nouns changing their vowels:

man	*men*
woman	*women*
foot	*feet*
goose	*geese*
mouse	*mice*
tooth	*teeth*

Nouns ending in f or lf:
Change the **f** to **v** and add –**es**.

leaf	*leaves*
calf	*calves*

Regular Nouns ending in y:
Change the **y** to –**ies**.

baby	*babies*
body	*bodies*

Nouns ending in f:
Some only add –s at the end.

belief	*beliefs*
chief	*chiefs*
cliff	*cliffs*
roof	*roofs*

Nouns ending in fe:
Change the **f** to **v** and add –**s**.

life	*lives*
wife	*wives*
knife	*knives*

Nouns adding a syllable:

child	*children*
ox	*oxen*

Compound nouns when hyphenated:
Add an –s to the most important word.

father-in-law	*fathers-in-law*
good-bye	*good-byes*

Nouns with the same singular and plural form:		**Nouns with only a plural form:**	
deer	*deer*		
fish	*fish*		*pants*
means	*means*		*jeans*
offspring	*offspring*	NO SINGULAR	*pajamas*
series	*series*		*shorts*
sheep	*sheep*		*trousers*
species	*species*		

Nouns that end with an s but are not plural (singular, non-count):		**All non-count nouns do not form the plural because they cannot be counted.**	
		oxygen	
news		water	
politics		sand	
mathematics		rain	
statistics	NO PLURAL	furniture	NO PLURAL
physics		education	
athletics		English	
		swimming	

The noun people:	
person	
	people/persons (mostly in legal contexts)
people	
(a body of persons sharing a common religion, culture, and language)	*peoples*

Nouns deriving from other languages:
Most of these words can be categorized according to their ending and the language they derive from, mainly Greek and Latin.

cactus	*cacti/cactuses*	analysis	*analyses*
fungus	*fungi*	basis	*bases*
nucleus	*nuclei*	crisis	*crises*
stimulus	*stimuli*	hypothesis	*hypotheses*
syllabus	*syllabi*	oasis	*oases*
		parenthesis	*parentheses*
criterion	*criteria*	bacterium	*bacteria*
phenomenon	*phenomena*	medium	*media*
		curriculum	*curricula*
appendix	*appendices/appendixes*		
index	*indices/indexes*		

NOUN TYPES

Nouns are further classified into different types according to their different properties. These properties determine how nouns function within sentences, especially with verbs, articles, and pronouns.

- Each noun type relies on a basic principle that can help determine the correct usage of the noun without a person having to memorize every noun in the English language. Instead, applying these principles can--for the most part--allow a person to use nouns correctly.

- These noun types are not mutually exclusive, so a noun may belong to more than one type.

- The types of nouns are the following: **Common, Proper, Count,** and **Non-count.**

Common Nouns

Definition	Example
Most nouns name **general,** non-specific persons, places, things, and ideas. These nouns are classified as *common* nouns.	*Persons*: student, instructor, professor, dean *Places*: class, room, quad, university *Things*: book, syllabus, chalk, blackboard *Ideas*: education, progress, inspiration, knowledge

Principle: *NON-SPECIFIC* persons, places, things, and ideas
Significance: article usage

Proper Nouns

Definition	Example
The nouns that name **specific** persons, places, things, or ideas are classified as *proper* nouns.	*Persons*: Jimmy, Dr. Vance, Prof. Briggs *Places*: Room 101, Riverside, the Bell Tower *Things*: Compass: Guidebook, Blackboard, Internet *Ideas*: English, Spanish, Chinese, Capitalism

Principle: *SPECIFIC* persons, places, things, and ideas
Significance: article usage, plurals, and capitalization

Count Nouns

Definition

Most nouns can be counted, and those that can are classified as *count* nouns. These nouns form both the singular and the plural, and they require a verb in either the singular or the plural accordingly.

Collective (Count) Nouns: this is a special sub-category of count nouns used to group persons, things, and places into one entity. Like count nouns, they can form both the singular and the plural. However, these nouns can be tricky: when the collective noun functions as one entity, *which happens in the majority of cases*, it is used in the singular and requires a verb in the singular; if it does not function as one unit, **which happens very rarely**, it is still used in the singular but requires a verb in the plural.

Principle: Nouns or their individual components *CAN* be counted.
Significance: singular and plural formation, pronoun usage, article usage, agreement

Example

Count Nouns

Persons: student(s), instructor(s), professor(s), dean(s)

Places: class(es), room(s), quad(s), university(ies)

Things: book(s), syllabus(i), desk(s), black-board(s)

Ideas: (ideas and abstract nouns usually can not be counted)

Collective (Count) Nouns

This class (of students) performs very well.

This class (of students) sit at individual desks.

Non-Count Nouns

Definition

The nouns that cannot be counted are classified as *non-count* nouns. These nouns cannot form the plural, and they always take their verb in the singular.

Mass (Non-Count) Nouns: these are fluids, solids, gases, particles, natural phenomena, or groups of similar items that usually *cannot be broken down into their constituent components* without some other form of measurement or unit expression. This ability to break down the noun into distinct components is the difference between mass nouns and collective nouns.

Example

Mass (Non-Count) Nouns

Fluids: water, gas, coffee

Solids: glass, paper, wood

Gases: oxygen, nitrogen, ozone

Particles: chalk, grass, sand

Natural Phenomena: weather, heat, gravity

Similar Items: equipment, furniture, machinery

(Continued)

Abstract (Non-Count) Nouns: these are nouns that cannot be perceived or experienced through the senses but can only be imagined or conceptualized through the mind. Most ideas, languages, fields of study, recreation, and activities belong in this category.

Abstract (Non-Count) Nouns

Ideas: education, intelligence, information

Languages: English, Spanish, Chinese

Fields of Study: chemistry, physics, mathematics

Recreation: tennis, baseball, basketball

Activities: studying, learning, competing

Principle: Nouns or their components *CANNOT* be counted.
Significance: singular and plural formation, pronoun usage, article usage, subject/verb agreement

---

Highlight Points:

A. **Counting Non-Count Nouns**

In order to count non-count nouns, you can use some form of measurement or unit expression.

*I would like **water** to drink. (**Non-Count**: Water here functions as a non-count noun because you are not counting the amount of water you are asking for.)*

*I would like **a glass of water**. (**Non-Count**: Water here is still non-count; however, the unit expression of **a glass** indicates how much water you are asking for. Then, you can **count** one or more **glasses** of water.)*

B. **Hybrid Count/Non-Count Nouns**

Some nouns seem to be both count and non-count. How is this possible? These exceptions depend on the context. Just remember and apply the principle: "can you count the noun or its parts in the context?"

*John started losing **hair** at the age of eighteen. (**Non-Count**: Can you count the individual hairs he lost? No.)*

*At the age of fifty, John is left with only two **hairs** on his head. (**Count**: Can you count the individual hairs? Yes.)*

C. **Concrete Nouns**

Some grammar texts include additional types such as "concrete nouns", and they separate mass nouns, collective nouns, and abstract nouns into different categories. However, this distinction does not affect the noun's grammatical function; therefore, it has been omitted from this book.

Traveling as Education

Few **people** directly connect **traveling** with **education**, but even if they do, the connection occurs primarily in the form of sightseeing, visiting museums such as the Louvre or the Metropolitan, sampling foreign cuisine, and of course gathering souvenirs. The education involved is often limited to what travelers acquire from a museum docent or a guidebook. Ultimately, the travelers return to their normal routines with a set of pictures and some stories to tell about strange architecture, strange foods, and strange people. Besides and beyond these aspects, however, traveling can be one of the most important contributing factors to a person's educational development. Under the right circumstances, traveling may prove to be equally necessary if not more enriching than schooling.

Practice with Nouns

1. Identify all the nouns (persons, places, things, or ideas) in the text by underlining them.

2. Make two separate columns: a) list all nouns in the singular—e .g. *education*; b) list all nouns in the plural—*e.g. people*.

3. Label each underlined noun according to its type. Remember that each noun could belong to more than one type (proper, count, non-count, etc.)— *e.g. people: common, count noun*.

4. Name all the nouns in your classroom, and classify them according to their types.

The Statue of Liberty

Proper Noun/Singular/Non-count

The Parthenon

Proper Noun/Singular/Non-count

Chapter One--Mini-Review: Nouns

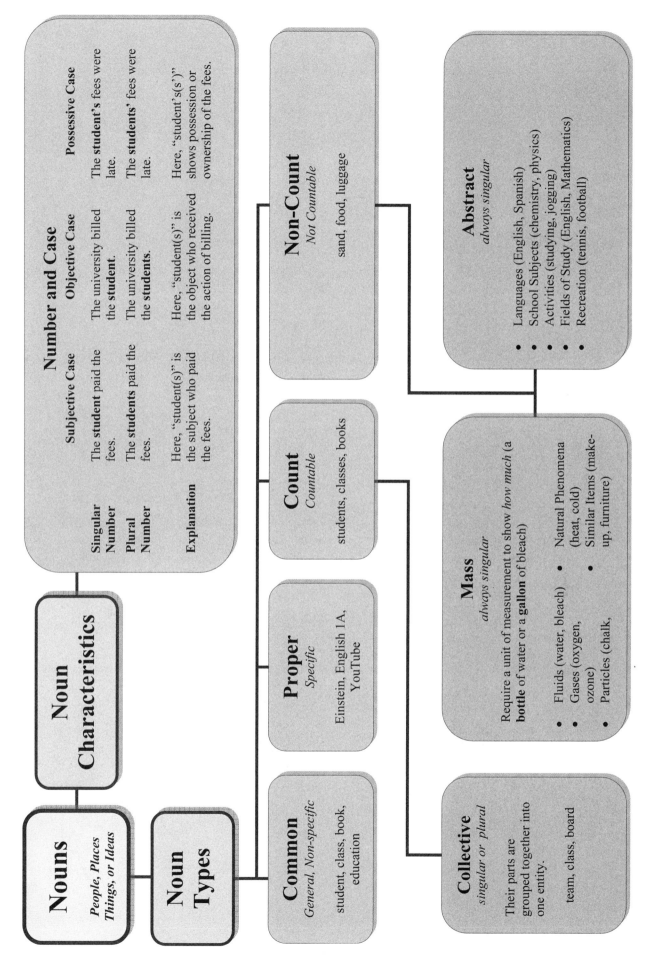

Nouns
People, Places Things, or Ideas

Noun Characteristics

Number and Case

	Subjective Case	Objective Case	Possessive Case
Singular Number	The **student** paid the fees.	The university billed the **student**.	The **student's** fees were late.
Plural Number	The **students** paid the fees.	The university billed the **students**.	The **students'** fees were late.
Explanation	Here, "student(s)" is the subject who paid the fees.	Here, "student(s)" is the object who received the action of billing.	Here, "student's(s')" shows possession or ownership of the fees.

Noun Types

Common
General, Non-specific

student, class, book, education

Proper
Specific

Einstein, English 1A, YouTube

Count
Countable

students, classes, books

Non-Count
Not Countable

sand, food, luggage

Collective
singular or plural

Their parts are grouped together into one entity.

team, class, board

Mass
always singular

Require a unit of measurement to show *how much* (a **bottle** of water or a **gallon** of bleach)

- Fluids (water, bleach)
- Gases (oxygen, ozone)
- Particles (chalk,
- Natural Phenomena (heat, cold)
- Similar Items (make-up, furniture)

Abstract
always singular

Languages (English, Spanish)
School Subjects (chemistry, physics)
Activities (studying, jogging)
Fields of Study (English, Mathematics)
Recreation (tennis, football)

PRONOUNS

PRONOUN DEFINITIONS

Formal Definition

<u>Form</u>: Pronouns are the words used to replace nouns. As with nouns, their form as singular or plural conveys information about their quantity or number while their position in the sentence conveys information about their function. The noun a pronoun refers to or replaces is called an *antecedent*.

<u>Function</u>: In a sentence, pronouns can function in many different ways, just like nouns. Pronouns can be subjects, objects, complements, and modifiers. Their specific function within the sentence determines the *case* of the pronoun (subjective, objective, possessive/ modifier).

<u>Etymology</u>: The word pro*noun* derives from the Latin words *pro* and *nomen*, meaning *for* and *name*. This is exactly what pronouns do: they substitute for nouns.

Informal Definition

As a director of a movie or a play, often times you have scenes that may be difficult to shoot. If you have Brad Pitt in the movie, for instance, you don't want him performing a death-defying stunt. Instead, you employ trained stunt doubles who take Brad Pitt's place. Also, if you have a tight budget for the place, you might not fly the whole film crew to England for a scene at the Buckingham Palace. Instead, you have your special effects crew construct a fake or simulated palace for the setting of your film or play. In this same way, pronouns take the place of nouns (persons, places, things, or ideas) by substituting for them.

Travelogue

June 10th, 2006

Greece, Crete, A Good Teacher

Having found **myself** an eager teacher at the bakery, I grasped the opportunity to learn a few more Greek terms. I had already learned the Greek noun for bread, "psomi", but I had to communicate to the sales assistant which bread I wanted. **She** pointed to two different kinds of bread and said, "*pio? Afto i ekino?*" I understood from the sign language that **she** was asking, "**Which? This** or **that?**" I realized that instead of repeating the noun "psomi" every time, **she** used the pronouns "**which**", "**this**", and "**that**" to substitute for **it**. Then, **she** said **something** confusing when **she** exclaimed with pride and pointed to **her** chest, "*Ego to eftiaxa*". **These** were words I had never heard before, but I knew **she** meant to say, "**I** made **it**". Two pronouns to add to **my** list: "*Ego*" **that** is "**I**" to refer to **oneself** when speaking and "*to*" **that** is "**it**" to refer to and substitute for the bread or a thing.

PRONOUN CHARACTERISTICS

Pronoun Number

Depending on their form, pronouns convey information about the number of the noun they substitute. Therefore, the noun the pronoun substitutes determines the pronoun's number.

> A **student** in the class arrived late today. **He** missed the whole exam. **(singular)**

> The **students** came to class early today. **They** were all prepared for the exam. **(plural)**

Pronoun Gender

Depending on their form, pronouns convey information about the gender of the noun they substitute.

> **John** arrived late today. **He** missed the whole **exam**. **It** is going to affect **his** grade.

Pronoun Person

Depending on their form, pronouns convey information about the person who speaks (first person: I, we, etc.), the person who is addressed (second person: you, you, etc), and the person or thing spoken of (third person: he, she, it, they, etc.).

> **I (first person)** usually procrastinate, but **you (second person)** always complete assignments on time.

Pronoun Case

Depending on their position in the sentence, pronouns convey information about their function as subjects (subjective case), objects (objective case), complements, or possessives (possessive case). Their form can change in some or all of the cases depending on the pronoun type.

> This instructor is an authority in her field; **she (subjective case)** is very knowledgeable, the textbook used in the class is **hers (possessive case)**, and students trust and admire **her (objective case)**.

PRONOUN TYPES

Pronouns are further classified into different types according to their different properties. These properties determine how pronouns function within sentences.

The types of pronouns are the following: **Personal, Intensive, Reflexive, Relative, Interrogative, De-**

monstrative, Reciprocal, and Indefinite.

Personal Pronouns

These pronouns substitute for or refer to specific nouns (antecedents). They vary in form to indicate person, number, gender, and case.

	Subjective Case	Objective Case	Possessive Case
		First Person	
Singular	I	me	mine, (my)
Plural	we	us	ours, (our)
Examples	**I/We** lost a book.	The instructor lent **me/us** a book.	The lost book is **mine/ours**. **(My/Our)** book is lost.
		Second Person	
Singular	you	you	yours, (your)
Plural	you	you	yours, (your)
Examples	**You/you** lost a book.	The instructor lent **you/you** a book.	The lost book is **yours/yours**. **(Your/Your)** book is lost.
		Third Person	
Singular	he/she/it	him/her/it	his/hers/(its), (his/her/its)
Plural	they	them	theirs, (their)
Examples	**He/She/It/They** lost a book.	The instructor lent **him/her/it/them** a book.	The lost book is **his/hers/(its)/theirs**. **(His/Her/Its/Their)** book is lost.

Highlight Points:

A. **Possessive Adjectives vs. Possessive Adverbs**

In other textbooks the possessive case of personal pronouns (my, your, his, her, its, their) is referred to as "possessive adjectives". In the examples provided, these possessive pronouns function as adjectives because they modify the following noun (for more see Parts of Speech: Adjectives).

B. **Possessive Case vs. Contractions**

Many times people confuse the possessive case of personal pronouns, especially *its* with *it's*, the truncated version *it is* or *it has*.

Intensive Pronouns

These pronouns refer to a preceding noun or pronoun and also end with –self or -selves. Intensive pronouns are **used either in the subjective or the objective case (rarely)**. As the term indicates, intensive pronouns are used to intensify the noun or pronoun they refer to.

Reflexive Pronouns

Similar to intensive pronouns, reflexive pronouns also refer back to a noun or pronoun and end with –self or –selves. However, reflexive pronouns are *used only in the objective case*. As the term indicates, *reflexive* pronouns are used *to reflect back* on the noun or pronoun they refer to.

	Subjective Case	Objective Case
First Person		
Singular	myself	myself
Plural	ourselves	ourselves
Examples	*Intensive* I **myself** /We **ourselves** lost the book.	*Reflexive* I/We blame **myself/ourselves** for losing the book.
Second Person		
Singular	yourself	yourself
Plural	yourselves	yourselves
Examples	*Intensive* You **yourself**/ You **yourselves** lost the book.	*Reflexive* You should blame **yourself/yourselves** for losing the book.
Third Person		
Singular	himself/herself/itself	himself/herself/itself
Plural	themselves	themselves
Examples	*Intensive* He/She/It/They **himself/herself/itself/themselves** lost the book.	*Reflexive* He/She/It should blame **himself/herself/itself/themselves** for losing the book.

Highlight Points:

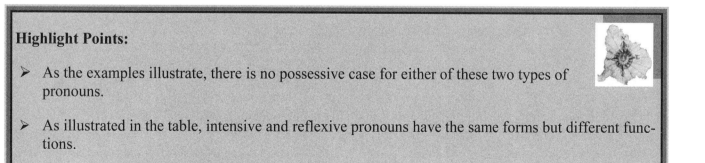

➤ As the examples illustrate, there is no possessive case for either of these two types of pronouns.

➤ As illustrated in the table, intensive and reflexive pronouns have the same forms but different functions.

Relative Pronouns

These pronouns refer to a preceding noun and introduce a new **dependent clause**. The characteristics of these pronouns are the following:

- **NUMBER**—the relative pronoun always reflects the number of the noun it refers to (antecedent) even if its form does not change.

    *The student **who** has lost the book is a junior, but the students **who** have found the book are seniors.*

- **GENDER**—the relative pronoun always reflects the gender of the noun it refers to (antecedent), and its form does change. **Who** and **that** refer to persons; **which** and **that** refer to places, things, and ideas.

    *The student **who/that** lost the book is a junior. The book **which/that** was lost was very expensive.*

- **PERSON**— the relative pronoun always reflects the person of the noun it refers to (antecedent) even if its form does not change.

    *You **who** are so careful should have never lost the book. Jerry **who** is so clever has memorized the book.*

- **CASE**— the relative pronoun does not always reflect the case of the noun it refers to (antecedent); instead, its case is determined by its own function in the relative dependent clause (subjective, objective, possessive case).

    *The students **who (subjective case)** lost the book will be punished. The students **whom (objective case)** you blamed denied losing the book. The instructor **whose (possessive case)** book was lost was furious.*

	Subjective Case	Objective Case	Possessive Case
Relative	who, whoever, what, whatever, which, whichever, that	whom, whomever, which, whichever, what, whatever, that	whose
Examples	The book **which** was valuable was lost.	The book **which** the student lost was valuable.	The student **whose** bag was stolen had the book in it.

Interrogative Pronouns

These pronouns observe the same changes as relative pronouns above, but they are used *exclusively* to introduce an interrogative *independent clause*, that is a question.

Who lost the book? Whom did the book belong to? Whose responsibility is it to find the book?

	Subjective Case	Objective Case	Possessive Case
Interrogative	Who, whoever, what, whatever, which, whichever?	Whom, whomever, which, whichever, what, whatever, that?	Whose?
Examples	**Which** book was lost?	**Which** book did the student lose?	**Whose** bag was stolen?

Highlight Points:

The form of relative and interrogative pronouns is the same. They only differ in their function as introducing relative (dependent) clauses or interrogative (independent) clauses (for more see Sentence Structures: Clauses).

Demonstrative Pronouns

These pronouns, unlike most pronouns, point out nouns that usually follow and not precede. Their form only changes to indicate number.

	Subjective Case	Objective Case
Singular	this/ that	this/that
Plural	these/those	these/those
Examples	**This** is the book the student lost. **That** is the student that lost the book.	Here, take **these**; they are the books the student lost.

Highlight Points:

A. Demonstrative Pronouns and Physical Location

If demonstrative pronouns point out something physically, then "this/these" are used for something that is nearby while "that/those" point out something that is further away.

B. Demonstrative Pronouns vs. Demonstrative Adjectives

Demonstrative pronouns are often used as adjectives that modify the noun that follows. Once more, this illustrates that the same word (form) can have different functions.

This is my book. *(Pronoun) This* book is mine. *(Adjective)*

Reciprocal Pronouns

These pronouns refer to the individual parts of a plural noun or pronoun that precedes (antecedent). Their form does not change, and they only appear in the objective case.

	Subjective Case	Objective Case
Singular	--	--
Plural	--	each other, one another
Examples	--	The students blamed **each other/one another** for losing the book.

Indefinite Pronouns

These pronouns refer to non-specific nouns. Their form does not change to show person, gender, and case. However, many of them are either singular or plural while other can be both.

Subjective or Objective Case

Singular	one, someone, everyone, anyone, no one/ somebody, everybody, anybody, no-body
	something, everything, anything, nothing/ each, much, either, neither, none
Plural	both, few, many, several
Singular/ Plural	all, most, more, some, any, either
Examples	**Someone** knows who lost the book.(**Singular**)
	Few know who lost the book. (**Plural**)
	All know who lost the book. (**Plural**)
	All I know is that I did not lose the book. (**Singular**)

Highlight Points:

Indefinite Pronouns and Agreement

➢ Indefinite pronouns can be difficult in terms of pronoun/antecedent agreement. Indefinite pronouns such as someone, anyone, nobody, etc. do not provide any information about the gender of that person.

➢ Indefinite pronouns are often confusing in subject/verb agreement. In both of these cases, consulting the chart on indefinite pronouns to know which indefinite pronouns are singular, plural, or both will help with avoiding errors.

Someone *gave me* ***his*** *book. (You should use "his" if you know the person is male).* *Someone* *left* ***their (his/her)*** *book in the classroom. (You should use "their" or "his/her" if you do not know the gender of the person).*

Travel Destinations

Defining traveling as education is of primary significance. Starting in a reverse way, **we** can define traveling by asking **this**, "what does not constitute traveling?" This does not necessarily involve a great distance to or a great length of time at the place of destination; it does not have to be a trip to Tibet or a year spent in the Australian Outback as a hermit. Traveling itself could be as simple as taking a bus trip to a nearby city to spend a Saturday morning. Thus, it mainly depends on the places of origin and of destination. Distance and time are not the issues; rather, what is more important is that travelers themselves should be exposed to new people and to an environment which is different than **theirs**. In that sense, traveling can stretch the fabric of what and whom we know, which exposes us to different experiences, cultures, and people. Therefore, if one is from a particular region in the U. S., journeying to a town ten miles down the road may not count. Though some of the landscape or the facilities may be different, most likely the essence of the place and the way one interacts with the environment remain the same. The way one shops for food will be more or less the same in the local supermarket, organized in a congruent way, having identical products, and overall the same modus operandi as one's place of origin. If the place of destination is then quite similar to the place of origin, the traveler will not be intrigued to reevaluate the environment and their place within it.

Practice with Pronouns

1. Identify all the pronouns in the text by underlining them. Then find the noun each pronoun replaces or refers to— *e.g. we-refers to the speaker/people in general.*

2. Make three separate columns: a) list all pronouns in the subjective case-- *e.g. we*; b) list all pronouns in the objective case--*e.g.this*, c) list all pronouns in the possessive case --*e.g. theirs.*

3. Label each underlined pronoun according to its type/person/ number/gender/case, if applicable— *e.g. we: personal pronoun/first person/singular/subjective case.*

4. Construct a paragraph that describes your classroom using as many pronouns as you can. Then, apply exercises 1-3 to your paragraph.

The Winding Road

It can lead you to new places.
Personal Pronoun/Singular/
Subjective Case

Chapter One--Mini-Review: Pronouns

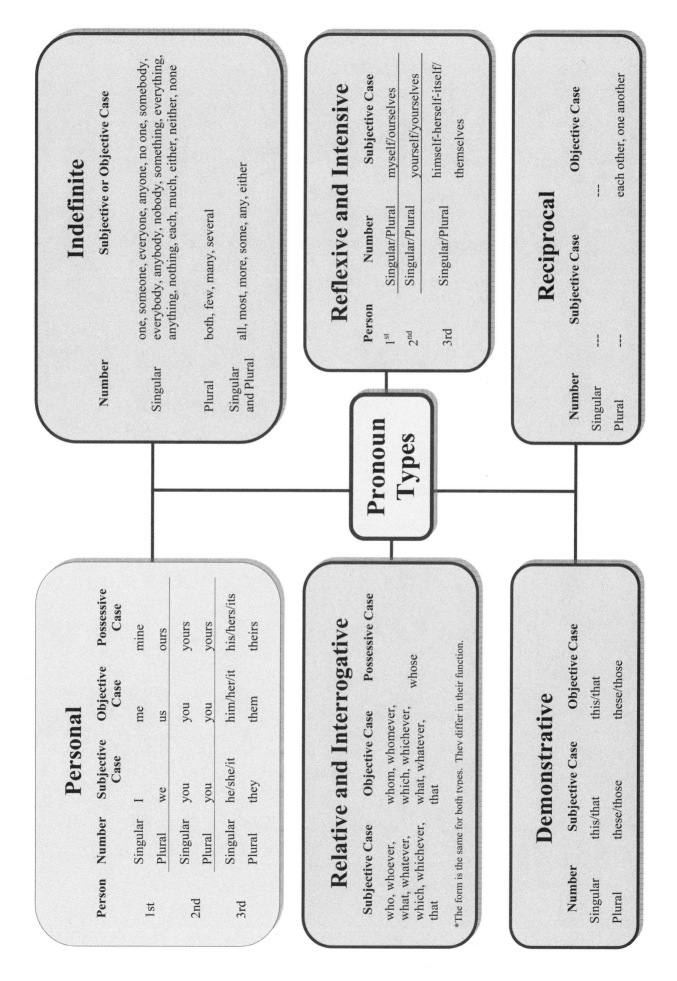

Pronoun Types

Personal

Person	Number	Subjective Case	Objective Case	Possessive Case
1st	Singular	I	me	mine
	Plural	we	us	ours
2nd	Singular	you	you	yours
	Plural	you	you	yours
3rd	Singular	he/she/it	him/her/it	his/hers/its
	Plural	they	them	theirs

Indefinite

Subjective or Objective Case

Number	
Singular	one, someone, everyone, anyone, no one, somebody, everybody, anybody, nobody, something, everything, anything, nothing, each, much, either, neither, none
Plural	both, few, many, several
Singular and Plural	all, most, more, some, any, either

Reflexive and Intensive

Person	Number	Subjective Case
1st	Singular/Plural	myself/ourselves
2nd	Singular/Plural	yourself/yourselves
3rd	Singular/Plural	himself-herself-itself/ themselves

Relative and Interrogative

Subjective Case	Objective Case	Possessive Case
who, whoever, what, whatever, which, whichever, that	whom, whomever, which, whichever, what, whatever, that	whose

*The form is the same for both types. They differ in their function.

Reciprocal

Number	Subjective Case	Objective Case
Singular	---	---
Plural	---	each other, one another

Demonstrative

Number	Subjective Case	Objective Case
Singular	this/that	this/that
Plural	these/those	these/those

ADJECTIVES

Form: Adjectives are the words that ***describe*** (***modify***) or ***specify*** (***limit***) nouns and pronouns.

- The adjectives used to describe nouns and pronouns do not change their form regardless of the number, case, gender, or person of the noun or the pronoun they describe (modify). They only change their form in terms of their ***degree of intensity*** (positive, comparative, superlative).

- On the other hand, adjectives used to specify (limit) nouns and pronouns often change their form to observe the characteristics of the nouns and pronouns they specify (limit).

Formal Definition

Function: In a sentence, adjectives always accompany a noun or pronoun.

- Sometimes adjectives are placed directly next to the noun or pronoun they describe (modify) or specify (limit). In this case, they function as modifiers.

  *The **diligent** student studied for the test. (adjective-modifier)*

- In other cases, they are connected to the noun or pronoun through a linking verb. In these cases, they function as subject complements.

  *This student is **diligent**. (adjective-subject complement)*

Etymology: The word adjective derives from the Latin words *ad + jacere*, meaning *to add to*. This is exactly what adjectives do: they add information about the noun or pronoun they accompany.

Informal Definition

Once the actors, the setting, the props, ideas, stunt doubles, and simulated scenery are in place, a director needs to transform all of them into something unique and specially related to the specific film. To accomplish that transformation, the director may use make-up and costumes to alter and modify the characteristics of actors. With the help of make-up, for instance, a twenty-year old actress may be modified to look like a sixty-year old woman. Likewise, the stage setting may be modified with fake snow to look like a mountainous region. In this same way, adjectives describe and specify nouns and pronouns.

Highlight Points:

English can be tricky. In many cases words that look like adjectives function as nouns and vice-versa. Therefore, it is always important to remember that despite the word's form, one needs to analyze its specific function within the specific context.

➢ Adjectives as Nouns:

The ***young*** *students all received "A's" in Chemistry.* ***(as adjective)***

The ***young*** *need to learn how to study.* ***(as noun)***

➢ Nouns as Adjectives:

Many times a diligent ***student*** *needs to make sacrifices.* ***(as noun)***

Many times ***student*** *responsibilities require sacrifices.* ***(as adjective)***

Travelogue

June 10th, 2006

Greece, Crete, Baking Adjectives

My first Greek grammar lesson at the bakery ended with adjectives. There were so many different kinds of bread: dark bread with sesame seeds; white bread with bits of cheese on top; bread with black olives; even bread in the shape of chickens. I had to tell the assistant the specific kind I wanted, but she suspected I needed additional help. At this point, the helpful assistant asked me "To aspro psomi?" pointing to a loaf of white bread with cheese. I assumed that "aspro" means "white", but I wanted the large, dark loaf of bread. Pointing at it, she responded understandingly, "ahh, to mavro psomi". "Mavro" then has to mean dark. The experience was interesting and the bread delicious.

ADJECTIVE CHARACTERISTICS:

Degrees of Intensity

Positive Degree	**Form**: This is the regular form of the adjective. **Function**: The positive degree of intensity is used simply to describe a noun or pronoun without any comparison. *The **large** handbook was rather expensive.*
Comparative Degree	**Form**: The comparative degree typically forms by adding either the –*er* ending or the words ***more***/***less*** to the positive degree form of the adjective. **Function**: The comparative degree of intensity is used to describe a noun or pronoun in comparison to another one. *A workbook is usually **larger** than a handbook.*
Superlative Degree	**Form**: The superlative degree of intensity typically forms by adding the article "the" and either the –*est* ending or the words ***most*** and ***least*** to positive degree form of the adjective. **Function**: The superlative degree of intensity is used to describe a noun or pronoun in comparison to two or more things of the same kind. *This handbook is the **largest** book I have ever used.*

Irregular Forms of Degrees of Intensity

Positive	Comparative	Superlative
good	better	best
bad	worse	worst
many	more	most
little	less	least
less	lesser	least
far (distance)	farther	farthest
far (extent)	further	furthest
ill	worse	worst

Highlight Points:

A. Describing (Modifying) vs. Specifying (Limiting)

Adjectives can be classified into two main groups: those that describe (modify) nouns and pronouns and those that specify (limit) nouns and pronouns. Only describing (modifying) adjectives have three different degrees of intensity: positive, comparative, and superlative.

B. Degrees of Intensity and Syllables

When to use *–er* or *more/ less*, and *-est* or *most/ least* for the comparative and superlative degrees:

➢ One-syllable adjectives usually take **–er** and **–est.**

   simple-simpler-simplest, high-higher-highest

➢ Two-syllable adjectives usually take either **–er/-est** or **more/less** and **most/least.**

   heavy-heavier-heaviest, complex-more complex-most complex

➢ Three-syllable adjectives take more/less and most/least.

   diligent-more diligent-most diligent, careful-more careful-most careful

ADJECTIVE TYPES

Descriptive (Modifying)

Definition	Example
These adjectives are used to describe nouns and pronouns. They do not change their form regardless of the number, case, gender, or person of the noun or the pronoun they describe (modify). They only change their form in terms of their degree of intensity (positive, comparative, superlative).	*Persons*: **brilliant** student(s), **interesting** instructor(s) *Places*: **small** class(es), **sunny** room(s) *Things*: **thick** book(s), **thorough** syllabus *Ideas*: **secondary** education, **impressive** progress

Specifying (Limiting)

These adjectives are used to specify (limit) nouns and pronouns. They change their form to observe the characteristics of the nouns and pronouns they specify (limit).

Sub Types	Example
Articles: a, an (indefinite article), the (definite article)	A brilliant student received **an** "A". **The** student then graduated with honors.
Demonstrative: this, these, that, those	**This** grammar book is really interesting. **Those** other grammar books are too complicated.
Indefinite: any, each, few, other, some, etc.	**Each** student received a laptop. **Some** students complained the laptops were defective.
Interrogative: what, which, whose?	**Which** instructor do you have for Chemistry? **What** test did you ace?
Numerical: one, first, two, second, etc.	My **first** quarter in college was the hardest.
Possessive: my, your, their, etc.	**Your** oral presentation was better than mine.
Relative: what, which, whose, whatever, etc.	**Whatever** decision you make, we'll be there.

Highlight Points:

A. Articles

➤ Form

- There are two types of articles, indefinite (a, an) and definite (the).

- The indefinite article (a, an) does not have a plural number.

- The definite article (the) has the same form for both the singular and the plural.

- "An" is used when the noun starts with a vowel sounding letter (*an hour, an apple*).

➤ Function

- The indefinite article is used to specify (limit) a single noun that is generic (non-specific).

  A student in my class is from China. (This means that one of the students in the class is from China, but we don't know which one specifically.)

- The definite article is used to specify (limit) a single or plural noun that is specific.

  The student in my class who is from China received an "A". (This means that there is a specific (non-generic) student who received an "A". He is specific because we know he is the one from China and not just anyone in the class.)

***For more information on articles, see Appendix: Articles.

B. Adjectives vs. Pronouns

Both interrogative and relative adjectives have the same form as interrogative and relative pronouns (see Parts of Speech: Pronouns). How can one determine when the same word is an adjective or a pronoun? Once more, it is the function of the word in the specific context that will determine what part of speech the word belongs to.

➤ Interrogative Adjectives vs. Interrogative Pronouns

  Which book is yours? (Interrogative Adjective: "which" specifies the noun "book")

  I have two books here. Which is yours? (Interrogative Pronoun: "which" introduces a question, and it does not accompany a noun or pronoun; it refers to the noun "books".)

➤ Relative Adjectives vs. Relative Pronouns

  Whichever the decision of our daughter, we'll be there to support her. (Relative Adjective: "whichever" specifies (limits) the noun "decision".)

  I know that my parents will be there to support my decision, whichever it is. (Relative Pronoun: "whichever" refers to and replaces the noun "decision".)

The Real Traveler

The real traveler should pursue not only exposure to an array of new stimuli but also an understanding of the differences and similarities among various places, people, and cultures. Indeed, genuine traveling goes beyond "seeing" a place to "understanding" that place. In that critical mode, traveling can broaden our cultural horizons, allowing us to see and seek to comprehend whatever ways the peoples of the world have. It can allow us to at least try to explain if not appreciate the multiple lenses in living and viewing life. Any act even as simple as eating ice cream could be interesting and instructive in that way. Indeed, some Americans would think nothing of purchasing an ice-cream cone from an ice-cream parlor and then strolling down the street. A similar action in Japan, on the other hand, would bring reproaching stares, for eating in public view is considered a low-class act of an uncultured person.

Practice with Adjectives

1. Identify all the adjectives in the text by underlining them. Then find the noun or pronoun each adjective describes (modifies) or specifies (limits)—*e.g. the- specifies (limits) the noun "traveler"; real- describes (modifies) the noun "traveler".*

2. Label each underlined adjective according to its type— *e.g. the: limiting adjective/definite article; real: descriptive adjective.*

3. For each adjective from the text, construct a chart that includes all its degrees of intensity (if possible)— *e.g. real (positive), more real (comparative), the most real (superlative).*

4. In the paragraph you have constructed about your classroom, try to identify all the adjectives you have used, and then try to add an adjective for every noun or pronoun in the paragraph. Then, apply exercises 1-3 to your paragraph.

Cultural Variety

Descriptive Adjective

Chapter One--Mini-Review: Adjectives

Adjective Types

Specifying (Limiting)

Relative and Interrogative
who, whose, what, which, whatever, whichever, whoever, etc.

Singular
- Whatever grade you earn comes from studying. (Relative)
- Which book did you select? (Interrogative)

Plural — same as singular

Possessive
my, your, his, her, its
- Your book is in my backpack.

our, your, their
- Our book is in your backpack.

Numerical
one, first, two, second, etc.
- The second volume is a masterpiece.

same as singular

Articles
a, an, the

Singular
- A student in my class studied (*one of many–Indefinite*).
- The best student in the class studied more hours (*one particular student–Definite*).

the

Plural
- The students in my class from Taiwan studied efficiently (*group of particular students– Definite*).

Demonstrative
this, that

Singular
- This student beside me studied all night (*location close by*).
- That student over by the stairs studied all night (*location farther away*).

these, those

Plural
- These students beside me studied all night (*location close by*).
- Those students over by the stairs studied all night (*location farther away*).

Indefinite
each
- Each student in the class studied many hours (*specifies the number of indefinite students*).

any, few, other, some
- Few students studied as much as they should have (*specifies the number*).

Descriptive (Modifying)

Degree of Intensity

	Positive (describes)	Comparative (compares)	Superlative ("the" most)
One Syllable	large	larger (add "*er*")	largest (add "*est*")
Two Syllable	heavy	heavier	heaviest
Three Syllable	diligent	more diligent	most diligent
Irregular	good	better	best

VERBS

Formal Definition

Form: Verbs are the words that adopt various forms to express time dimensions (past, present, future), time circumstances (repetition, in-progress, completion, duration), mood or state of their subjects. However, not all forms of verbs actually function as predicates in a sentence (for more see Parts of Speech: Verb Forms).

Function: Verbs are used to express action (somebody is doing something), occurrence (something is happening), or state of being (somebody or something is in a certain situation). They are the main building blocks of a sentence without which a sentence cannot exist.

Etymology: The word *verb* derives from the Latin word *verbum facere*, meaning to speak or make words. This is exactly what verbs do: they speak for their subjects.

Informal Definition

"Action!" This is the command that sets a movie or play in motion. While gathering together and transforming all the actors, scenery, and stunt doubles is incredibly important in directing a film, it is equally important that the actors do something (action), that something happens (occurrence) in the plot, or that an emotion is expressed (state of being). In this same way, verbs are the words that describe action, occurrence, and state of being in the past, present, and the future.

Action	Occurrence	State of Being
They *are dancing*.	Flowers *bloom*.	This cat *seems* relaxed!

Travelogue

June 10th, 2006

The Island of Crete, Greece

Hi Paul,

Walking down the street of old town Chania today with a loaf of bread in hand, I **whistled** (action) and **sung** (action). Oh! I also **learned** (action) my first five Greek words earlier today: "*psomi*" for bread, "*aspro*" for white, "*mavro*" for dark, "*ego*" for I, and "*afto*" for it; so, now I

feel (state of being) quite competent in Greek; at least, I **will not starve** (state of being). Trips **are** (state of being) so eventful and interesting: things **happen** (occurrence), you **meet** (action) new people, you **see** (action) extraordinary things, and you **experience** (state of being) so many emotions. I **am** utterly excited (state of being). As I **was walking** (action) through the cobble stone streets this morning, it **sprinkled** (occurrence) some, and the streets **smelled** (state of being) fresh and renewed. It **occurred** (occurrence) to me that I **had not felt** (state of being) so carefree for a long time.

VERB CHARACTERISTICS:

Verb Person	Verbs may change their form to convey information about the person who speaks (**First Person**: I act, we act), the person who is addressed (**Second Person**: you act, you act, etc.), and the person or thing spoken of (**Third Person**: *he/she/it acts*, they act).
Verb Number	Verbs may change their form to convey information about the number of their subject. Therefore, verbs can be **singular** or **plural**.
Verb Tense	Verbs may change their form to convey information about the time of the action, occurrence, or state of being. Verb tenses reflect the **past**, the **present**, and the **future**.
Verb Mood	Verbs may change their form to convey information about the "mood" their subject is in. This mood can be **indicative** (You run everyday.), **imperative** (Run!), **subjunctive** (If you run, you can catch the bus.).
Verb Voice	Verbs may change their form to convey information about the active or passive condition of their subject. This voice can be **active** (The student dropped the book.) or **passive** (The book was dropped by the student.).

Highlight Points:

Verb Person

Verbs usually do not change their form regardless of the person of their subject. The only change their form observes is in the third person singular of the Simple Present Tense. That is when an –s (or –es) ending is added to the main form of the verb (for more see Parts of Speech: Verb Forms).

*Any professor **conducts** experiments in class. Professors usually **conduct** experiments in class.*

VERB TYPES

Verbs are classified into different types according to their different properties. These properties determine how verbs function within sentences. However, these types are not mutually exclusive. The verb types are the following: **Main, Auxiliary, Linking, Transitive,** and **Intransitive**.

Main Verbs

Definition	Example
They are the verbs that show action, occurrence, or state of being in a clause or a sentence. They can consist of one or more words.	**Action**: During finals' week, students **study** the most. **Occurrence**: During finals' week, stress levels **rise**. **State of Being**: During finals' week, students **seem** exhausted.

Auxiliary (Helping) Verbs

Definition	Example
	Auxiliary verbs that help with tense: ▪ to be: This student *is* **speaking** right now. ▪ to have: This student *has* **spoken** once. ▪ to do: This student *does* **not speak** in class.
They are the verbs that help other verbs form tense, mood, or voice.	**Auxiliary verbs that help with mood (Modal Verbs):** can, could, may, might, will, would, shall, should, must ▪ This student *can* **speak** three languages. ▪ This student is so shy that he *might* **not speak** in class. **Auxiliary verbs that help with (passive) voice:** ▪ to be: This instructor *is* always **spoken** of with admiration.

Linking Verbs

Definition	Example

Linking verbs that show state of being or becoming:

They are the verbs that link (connect) a subject to a complement. They operate as equal signs (=) in an equation between the subject and its complement.

A complement, whether it be a noun, an adjective, a pronoun, or a clause, completes the subject in some way.

to appear, to seem, to get, to grow, to turn, to remain, etc.

- to be: My brother **is** a very smart freshman.

- to become: I **become** better every day thanks to this book.

Linking verbs that deal with the senses:

- to look: This student **looks** tired.

- to smell: This classroom **smells** moldy.

- to feel: Knowing grammar **feels** good.

- to sound: Some grammatical terms **sound** complicated.

- to taste: Cafeteria food **tastes** terrible.

Transitive Verbs

Definition	Example

They are the verbs that require an object to complete their meaning.

The energy of these verbs is **transferred** to their object.

The students **completed** their tests.

*The energy of the verb "**completed**" is **transferred** to the object "**tests**".*

The professor **graded** the papers.

*The energy of the verb "**graded**" is **transferred** to the object "**papers**".*

Intransitive Verbs

Definition	Example

They are the verbs that do not require an object to complete their meaning.

The energy of these verbs remains within the verb and its subject; it is **not transferred** to an object (for more see Sentence Structures: Predicates)

The professor **stayed** after class to talk to a student.

*The energy of the verb "stayed" is **not transferred** to an object; it remains within the verb and its subject.*

The students **sat** still in their desks.

*The energy of the verb "sat" is **not transferred** to an object; it remains within the verb and its subject.*

Highlight Points:

Hybrid Transitive/Intransitive Verbs

Some verbs can function as both transitive and intransitive. It all depends on whether in the particular case they need to transfer their energy to an object or not.

*I **see** the student who is falling asleep on his desk. (**Transitive**)*

*I **cannot see** without my glasses. (**Intransitive**)*

VERB FORMS

Verbs have six different forms: the **Base Form**, the **Simple Present Form (–s)**, the **Past Tense Form (-ed)**, the **Past Participle Form (-ed)**, the **Present Participle Form (-ing)**, and the **Infinitive Form (to-)**. Each one of these forms can perform various functions in a sentence.

The Base Form

Form	Function
This is the most basic and common or "dictionary" form of a verb.	This form, as its name indicates, is the **basis** for all other verb forms. It can stand on its own and function as a verb (e.g. see Simple Present Tense), or it can help mold other verb tenses or forms.
	Students often **talk** to their instructors about homework.
talk	*Here, "talk" is in the Base Form and functions as a verb-first person plural of the Simple Present Tense.*

The Simple Present Tense Form: (–s Form)

Form	Function
This verb form derives from the Base Form with the ending **—s.**	This form always functions as a verb and is used to indicate the Third Person Singular, Indicative Mood of the Simple Present Tense.
	Every week the instructor **talks** to the students about grammar issues.
talk—s	*Here, "talks" is in the Simple Present Tense (–s) Form and functions as a verb-third person singular of the Simple Present Tense.*

The Simple Past Tense Form: (–ed Form)

Form	Function
This verb form derives from the Base Form with the ending **—ed.**	This form always functions as a verb and is used to indicate the Simple Past Tense of regular verbs.
	Yesterday the instructor **talked** to the students about grammar issues.
talk—ed	*Here, "talked" is in the Simple Past Tense (–ed) Form and functions as a verb in the Simple Past Tense.*

The Past Participle Form: (–ed Form)

Form	Function
This verb form derives from the Base Form with the ending —**ed**.	**With an auxiliary verb**, this form creates various verb tenses (Present Perfect Tense, Past Perfect Tense, etc.), and it functions as a verb.
	The instructor **has** already *talked* to the students about this grammar issue.
	Here, "talked" is in the Past Participle (-ed) form and with the auxiliary verb "has" creates the Present Perfect Tense and functions as a verb.
	Without an auxiliary verb, this form functions as an adjective.
talk—ed	This already **talked**-about grammar issue is still very difficult to understand.
	Here, "talked" is in the Past Participle (–ed) Form, and without an auxiliary verb it functions as an adjective to modify the noun "issue".

The Present Participle Form: (–ing Form)

Form	Function
This verb form derives from the Base Form with the ending —**ing**.	**With an auxiliary verb**, this form creates various verb tenses (Present Progressive Tense, Past Progressive Tense, etc.), and it functions as a verb.
	Right now the instructor **is** *talking* to the students about grammar issues.
	Here, "talking" is in the Present Participle (–ing) Form, and with the auxiliary verb "is" it functions as a verb in the Present Progressive Tense.
	Without an auxiliary verb, this form functions as a noun (gerund) or as an adjective.
talk—ing	**Talking** about grammar issues is necessary for language development. *Here, "talking" is in the Present Participle (-ing) Form, and without an auxiliary verb it functions as a noun (gerund); it names an idea.*
	The **talking** students explained the concept thoroughly.
	Here, "talking" is in the Present Participle (-ing) Form, and without an auxiliary verb it functions as an adjective that describes (modifies) the noun "students".

The Infinitive Form: (to- Form)

Form	Function
This verb form derives from the Base Form preceded by the preposition "to-".	This form never functions as a verb. Instead, it can function as a noun, an adjective, or an adverb.
	As a noun: **To talk** to the instructor is often difficult for students. *Here, "to talk" is in the Infinitive Form and functions as a noun; it names an idea.* **As an adjective:** The reason **to talk** in class is the improvement of students' understanding of the material. *Here, "to talk" is in the Infinitive Form and functions as an adjective that describes (modifies) the noun "the reason".* **As an adverb:** The students are too shy **to talk**. *Here, "to talk" is in the Infinitive Form and functions as an adverb that modifies the adjective "shy."*
to talk	

Form	Verb	Example
Base Form	borrow	Good students always **borrow** extra books. (***verb***)
The Simple Present Tense (-s) Form	borrow-s	He **borrows** two books every week. (***verb***)
The Simple Past Tense (-ed) Form	borrow-ed	He **borrowed** fifty books last year. (***verb***)
The Past Participle (-ed) Form	borrow-ed	By April, he **had** already **borrowed** twenty books. (***part of verb***) The **borrowed** books have to be returned on time. (***adjective***)
The Present Participle (-ing) Form	borrow-ing	He **is borrowing** a James Joyce book right now. (***part of verb***) **Borrowing** books requires responsibility. (***noun***) He has an excellent **borrowing** record. (***adjective***)
The Infinitive Form	to borrow	**To borrow** books requires responsibility. (***noun***) The books **to borrow** are marked with a sticker. (***adjective***) He is too lazy **to borrow** books. (***adverb***)

Highlight Points:

A. Regular vs. Irregular Verbs

The Simple Past Tense Form takes –ed when the verb is regular. Irregular verbs also have a Simple Past Tense Form, but most times they do not take –ed to create this form. To be certain about this form of a verb, one needs to consult a dictionary or see Appendix: Irregular Verbs.

- *This student **speaked** too fast.* ***(Incorrect Simple Past Tense Form)***
- *This student **spoke** too fast.* ***(Correct Simple Past Form)***

B. The Simple Past Form (-ed) vs. Past Participle Form (-ed)

➤ Although the Simple Past Tense Form (-ed) and the Past Participle Form (-ed) often appear to be the same with regular verbs, their function is different. Therefore, to avoid confusion when one identifies these parts of speech, one needs to look at the function of the verb form.

- *The committee **discussed** the issue until they made a final decision.*
  ***(Simple Past Form**—functions as a **verb** because it expresses an action)*
- *The **discussed** issue came to a close when the final decision was made.*
  ***(Past Participle Form**—functions as an **adjective** because it modifies the noun "issue")*
- *The committee **has discussed** the issue, but they have not made a final decision yet.*
  ***(Past Participle Form**—functions as **part of a verb** with the auxiliary verb "has" and expresses an action)*

➤ The Simple Past Tense Form and the Past Participle Form often differ in the case of irregular verbs.

- *I **wrote** a two-page paper in one hour.* ***(Simple Past Tense Form)***
- *I have never **written** a two-page paper in one hour.* ***(Past Participle Form)***

C. Issues with the Present Participle Form (-ing)

➤ The Present Participle Form (-ing) may sometimes create confusion because it can function as part of a verb, an adjective, or a noun (gerund). Therefore, to avoid confusion when one identifies these parts of speech, one needs to look at the function of the verb form. Also, one needs to look for any auxiliary verbs, which indicate that the present participle is part of a verb.

- *The committee **is discussing** the issue right now.*
  ***(Present Participle Form**—functions as **part of a verb** with the auxiliary "is," and it expresses an action)*
- *The committee **discussing** the issue came to a final decision.*
  ***(Present Participle Form**—functions as an **adjective** because it modifies the noun "committee")*
- ***Discussing** issues always takes all day.*
  ***(Present Participle Form**—functions as a **noun** (gerund) because it names the idea of discussion)*

D. Verbals

Some grammar books refer to the Past Participle Form, the Present Participle Form, and the Infinitive Form of the verb as *Verbals*. For the purpose of this grammar book, these verb forms are categorized according to their functions; since those functions differ, they are not all grouped under a single category.

Cultural Exposure

Traveling **exposes** people to these alternative ways of viewing the world even if people just realize that not everyone reacts to situations with the same set of culturally ingrained codes. By frequent exposure to alternative methods of dealing with the world, people learn to approach differences and conflicts with expansive background knowledge. The man who seems utterly cold and silent at the first meeting is not necessarily rude. Instead, his behavior shows respect by listening intently to the speaker. The woman who "crowds" others in the grocery store line, violating their personal space, is perhaps following a behavior learned in her home country. Perhaps she has not adapted to her new environment. Rather than seeing these behaviors as "strange, weird, or rude", the real traveler is able to find them different yet normal. Thus, frequent travel ameliorates cultural conflicts through better understanding.

Practice with Verbs

1. Identify all the verbs in the text by underlining them. Then categorize these verbs according to their function (action, occurrence, state of being)—*e.g. exposes- action.*

2. Label each underlined verb according to its type (main, auxiliary, linking, transitive, intransitive)— *e.g. exposes: main/transitive.*

3. a) Make a chart with all verb forms (base, -s, -ed, etc.). b) Categorize each verb form in the text accordingly. c) Complete the chart for each verb form from the text— *e.g. exposes:-s form/expose: base form/exposed: simple past (-ed) form, etc.*

4. In the paragraph you have constructed about your classroom, try to identify all the verbs you have used and then try to apply exercises 1-3 to your paragraph.

The Monk *prays*

Main Verb

Cretan dancers *seem* happy

Linking Verb

Chapter One--Mini-Review: Verbs

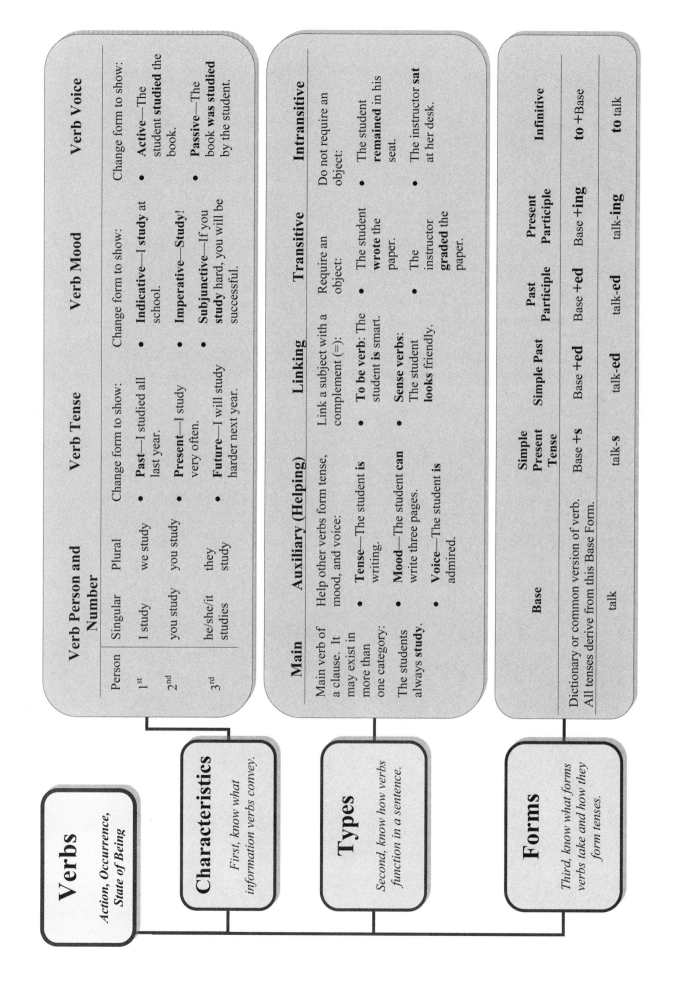

Verbs

Action, Occurrence, State of Being

Characteristics

First, know what information verbs convey.

Verb Person and Number

Person	Singular	Plural
1st	I study	we study
2nd	you study	you study
3rd	he/she/it studies	they study

Verb Tense

Change form to show:

- **Past**—I studied all last year.
- **Present**—I study very often.
- **Future**—I will study harder next year.

Verb Mood

Change form to show:

- **Indicative**—I **study** at school.
- **Imperative**—**Study**!
- **Subjunctive**—If you **study** hard, you will be successful.

Verb Voice

Change form to show:

- **Active**—The student **studied** the book.
- **Passive**—The book was **studied** by the student.

Types

Second, know how verbs function in a sentence.

Main

Main verb of a clause. It may exist in more than one category:

The students always **study**.

Auxiliary (Helping)

Help other verbs form tense, mood, and voice:

- **Tense**—The student **is** writing.
- **Mood**—The student **can** write three pages.
- **Voice**—The student **is** admired.

Linking

Link a subject with a complement (=):

- **To be verb**: The student **is** smart.
- **Sense verbs**: The student **looks** friendly.

Transitive

Require an object:

- The student **wrote** the paper.
- The instructor **graded** the paper.

Intransitive

Do not require an object:

- The student **remained** in his seat.
- The instructor **sat** at her desk.

Forms

Third, know what forms verbs take and how they form tenses.

Base	Simple Present Tense	Simple Past	Past Participle	Present Participle	Infinitive
Dictionary or common version of verb. All tenses derive from this Base Form.	Base +**s**	Base +**ed**	Base +**ed**	Base +**ed**	Base +**ing**	to +Base
talk	talk-**s**	talk-**ed**	talk-**ed**	talk-**ed**	talk-**ing**	to talk

ADVERBS

Formal Definition

Form: Adverbs are typically formed by adding an **–ly** to the end of an adjective. Their form also changes to express different degrees of intensity.

Function: Adverbs are the words used to modify verbs, adverbs, adjectives, or whole clauses. In a clause, adverbs can accompany verbs, adverbs, adjectives, or clauses to modify them. Adverbs typically convey information about manner (how?), place (where?), time (when?), degree of intensity (to what degree?), quantity (how much?), or frequency (how often?).

Etymology: The word *adverb* derives from the Latin words *ad* and *verbum*, meaning *to(ward)* and *word* accordingly. This is exactly what adverbs do: they accompany certain words (neither nouns nor pronouns) to modify them.

Informal Definition

*Once the scene has been set, the actors summoned, and the word "Action!" called, a director needs to step in and regulate what is happening on stage. Movies don't make themselves. Therefore, the director may, for instance, make changes in the way an actor walks across the stage (manner). She may say, "You need to walk **quickly**. No, **faster**. Yes, **always** walk like this." In this way, the director modifies how exactly things are done on the set. In this same way, adverbs modify verbs, adjectives, and other adverbs.*

Manner	Degree of Intensity	Frequency
The balloon fell *abruptly*.	The bee is *very* industrious.	This cat *always* hides!

Travelogue

June 16th, 2006.

The Lighthouse in Old Chania

Laboriously (manner) and painstakingly (manner) this lighthouse came to existence with stones and boulders slowly (manner) hauled and skillfully (manner) chiseled from the surrounding countryside. Ever since the 1570s, this lighthouse has silently (manner) stood as a sentinel to the Chanian harbor, a beacon to the lonely (adjective) seaman. Often (time) threatened with destruction by conquerors, earthquakes, and erosion, the lighthouse has persistently (degree of intensity) and stolidly (manner) defied them all. Historically (time) marking centuries of traditions, legends, and battles, this lighthouse proudly (manner) greets thousands of visitors every year, a physical reminder of the connection of the past to the present. Obviously (manner), it's needless to say how thrilling it is to view such a landmark from your hotel room.

ADVERB TYPES

Descriptive Adverbs

These adverbs are used to modify verbs, adverbs, adjectives, and clauses. They show manner (how?), place (where?), time (when?), degree of intensity (to what degree?), quantity (how much?), frequency (how often?).

Type	Example
Manner (How?)	The student completed the quiz **quickly**. *The adverb "quickly" refers to (modifies) the verb "completed", and it describes how (in what manner) the student completed the quiz.*
Place (Where?)	High school graduates take their SATs **locally**. *The adverb "locally" refers to (modifies) the verb "take", and it describes where (at which place) the high school graduates take their SATs.*
Time (When?)	High school graduates take their SATs **early**. *The adverb "early" refers to (modifies) the verb "take", and it describes when (at what time) the high school graduates take their SATs.*
Degree of Intensity (To what degree?)	The students completed the quiz **very** quickly. *The adverb "very" refers to the adverb (modifies) "quickly", and it describes the degree of intensity of this adverb.*
Quantity (How much?)	The students' answers to the SAT were **mostly** correct. *The adverb "mostly" refers to (modifies) the adjective "correct", and it describes how correct the answers were.*
Frequency (How often?)	This student **usually** completes quizzes quickly. *The adverb "usually" refers to (modifies) the verb "completes", and it describes how often the student completes quizzes quickly.*

Conjunctive (Descriptive) Adverbs

These adverbs are a subcategory of descriptive adverbs, but they are often treated differently because they modify independent clauses and show their relationship to the preceding clause.

The relationship they indicate may vary (addition, comparison/contrast, result/summary, time, emphasis, etc.). Many times conjunctive adverbs help **transition** from one clause to the other.

Conjunctive adverbs **should not be confused with conjunctions** although they sound similar. Conjunctive adverbs **do not connect clauses**; they **only help transition** logically from one clause to the other. On the other hand, conjunctions do connect clauses. This is significant when it comes to sentence errors such as comma splices and run-on sentences (for more see Sentence Structures: Sentence Types).

Type	Example
Addition: also, furthermore, moreover, besides **Contrast**: however, still, nevertheless, conversely, nonetheless, instead, otherwise **Comparison**: similarly, likewise **Result or Summary**: therefore, thus, consequently, accordingly, hence, then **Time**: next, then, meanwhile, finally, subsequently, indeed, certainly	The students **barely** studied. **However**, they still received good grades on their tests. *The word "barely" operates as a normal descriptive adverb that describes the intensity of the verb "studied". . The word "however" is a descriptive conjunctive adverb that refers to (modifies) the clause "they still...tests". Furthermore, "however" contrasts the two clauses and helps transition between them.* There was a fire in the dormitory on campus. **Consequently**, the students studied for final exams in the library. *The word "subsequently" is a descriptive conjunctive adverb that refers to (modifies) the clause "the students...library". Furthermore, "consequently" creates a relationship of result between the two clauses. It does not connect the two clauses grammatically as a conjunction would do; instead, it only helps transition between them.*

Relative Adverbs

These adverbs are words such as where, why, when, and their derivatives (whenever, wherever, etc.). They are used to introduce adjective dependent clauses (and sometimes noun dependent clauses; for more see Chapter Three: Sentence Structures: Clause Types). These clauses, then, function as adjectives that modify a noun or a pronoun by providing more information about it. **In essence, relative adverbs are adverbs, but the clauses they introduce function as adjectives**.

These relative adverbs **should not be confused** with the subordinating conjunctions that have the same form but different functions. The subordinating conjunctions (when, where, etc.) are used to introduce an adverb dependent clause (for more see Chapter Three: Sentence Structures: Clause Types). These clauses, then, function as adverbs that modify an entire clause.

Relative Adverb	Subordinating Conjunction
The time **when** I was a student in Germany was full of new experiences.	**When** I was a student in Germany, I had many new experiences.
*The word "**when**" here is a relative adverb. It introduces a whole clause which describes the noun "time" (which time? "The time **when** I was in Germany").*	*The word "**when**" here is a subordinating conjunction. It introduces a whole clause which functions as an adverb of time to the following clause. (When did you have many new experiences? "**When** I was a student in Germany").*
In most cases, a relative adverb can be replaced by the relative pronoun "that": "The time that I was a student in Germany was full of new experiences."	

Highlight Points:

A. Adverb Forms Without "-ly"

➤ Not all adverbs are formed by adding an "–ly" at the end of the adjective. There are many adverbs that do not even end with an "–ly". To make sure that a word is an adverb, one needs to see if it answers any of the adverb questions (when? where? how? etc.). Therefore, one needs to examine not only its form but also its function.

>   *very, well, always, often, here, there, much, etc.*

➤ In some instances, words that end with an "–ly" are not adverbs but adjectives. In these cases, again, one can identify what the word is by its function in the sentence (does it modify a noun or a pronoun? Adjective. Does it modify a verb, adverb, adjective, or clause? Adverb).

>   *Some **friendly** instructors greet their students when they enter the classroom.*

>   *The word "friendly" refers to and describes the noun "instructors"; therefore, because of its function it is an adjective.*

B. Adverbs and Degrees of Intensity

➤ The adverbs more/less and most/least are used as mentioned in the Adjectives section to form the degrees of intensity (comparative/superlative) of adjectives.

>   *An "A" paper is **more** thorough and analytical than a "B" paper.*

>   *The adverb "more" modifies the adjectives "thorough" and "analytical" and conveys information about their degree of intensity.*

➤ Like adjectives, adverbs are also characterized by three degrees of intensity: positive, comparative, and superlative. These degrees are formed for each adverb with the help of the endings "-er" and "-est" or with the help of "more/less" and "most/least" and the adverb.

- *Students who work **hard** are more likely to succeed. (**Positive Degree**)*

    *"A" students usually work **harder** than others. (**Comparative Degree**)*

    *Students who work **the hardest** are the ones who prosper in the class. (**Superlative Degree**)*

- *Students who work **intensively** are successful. (**Positive Degree**)*

    *"A" Students work **more intensively** than others. (**Comparative Degree**)*

    *Students who work the **most intensively** always succeed. (**Superlative Degree**)*

Stereotypes Suspended

When traveling, one should try to leave their preconceptions behind. **Therefore**, true traveling involves the suspension—to some degree--of one's own cultural values and expectations. It is precisely because many people who travel abroad often fail to do this that so many stereotypes of tourists exist. The "ugly American" is a famed stereotype of the wealthy tourist who always expects and demands that everything be like it is in the U.S. Loudly and obnoxiously, this stereotypical American tourist is constantly complaining about small sizes, limited English, and "inferior" service. However, Americans are not alone in these stereotypes. The Japanese are supposed to be obsessively glued to their cameras while the British are seen as snobby and condescending. While these stereotypes certainly exaggerate to one degree or another, they also teach an important lesson. Those tourists who personify these very well-known types of travelers have not only packaged their clothes and camera gear with them but also a tight set of cultural values and lenses, expecting that their world should be replicated anywhere they go. They are locked, consequently, into seeing the world in only one way and transforming it whenever possible. Such travel merely changes the architecture and the climate; it does not change the way in which these travelers view the world. So, why not save the money, stay at home, and watch a show on the Travel Channel?

Practice with Adverbs

1. Identify all the adverbs in the text by underlining them. Then, find the words (verbs, adjectives, adverbs, clauses) these adverbs refer to and modify— *e.g. therefore: it refers to the whole clause it introduces transitioning from the previous one.*

2. Label each underlined adverb according to its type (manner, place, time, conjunctive, etc.)— *e.g. therefore: (descriptive) conjunctive adverb.*

3. In the paragraph you have constructed about your classroom, try to identify all the adverbs you have used and then try to add more adverbs to further modify your verbs, adjectives, adverbs, or clauses. Last, try to apply exercises 1-2 to your paragraph.

Maro *always* smiles

Adverb of Frequency

Chapter One--Mini-Review: Adverbs

Adverbs

They modify verbs, adverbs, adjectives, and clauses.

Descriptive

Descriptive adverbs provide more information about the circumstances of a verb, an adjective, or another adverb. The following types of adverbs can be substituted into the sentence below to provide a slightly different context.

The students completed quizzes _____ .

quickly	*locally*	*early*	*very*	*entirely*	*frequently*
			efficiently		
Manner (how?)	**Place (where?)**	**Time (when?)**	**Degree of Intensity (degree?)**	**Quantity (how much?)**	**Frequency (how often?)**

Conjunctive

Conjunctive adverbs should not be confused with conjunctions. They **do not connect** clauses; they function as **transitional devices** and modify a whole clause.

The students completed the quiz; (Conjunctive Adverb), _____ .

furthermore, they had all the answers right.	**however,** they had many answers wrong.	**similarly,** they also finished their homework early.	**therefore,** they were able to leave school early.	**next,** many students began preparing for their next class.
Addition	**Contrast**	**Comparison**	**Result**	**Time**
also, moreover, besides	*still, nevertheless, conversely, nonetheless, instead*	*likewise*	*thus, consequently, accordingly, hence, then*	*then, meanwhile, finally, subsequently, indeed, certainly*

Relative

(When, Where, Why, etc.)

Relative adverbs introduce clauses that function as adjectives (Adjective Dependent Clauses). These clauses modify nouns or pronouns.

The year **when** I was a student in Germany was very interesting.

CONJUNCTIONS

CONJUNCTION DEFINITIONS

Formal Definition

Form: Conjunctions are the words that join various other words or groups of words, and their form does not change regardless of their function. They take the form of **Coordinating Conjunctions**, **Subordinating Conjunctions**, and **Correlative Conjunctions**.

Function: Conjunctions are used to join different elements such as words, phrases, clauses. They convey information about different relationships (cause/effect, result, time, etc.) among the elements they connect. In the case of clauses, they also are responsible for creating relationships of dependence or independence (for more see Sentence Structures: Sentence Type).

Etymology: The word *conjunction* derives from the Latin word *com + jungere*, meaning *together + to join*. This is exactly what conjunctions do: they join two or more elements.

Informal Definition

Once the various scenes of a movie have been shot, the director needs to work with the editor to decide how all these scenes will be connected. There are various ways to connect and to transition from scene to scene. The director can decide to "fade in or out" from a scene in which the screen steadily goes black. She may decide to "cross fade" in which the pictures from both scenes appear simultaneously on the screen. She may simply "cut" directly to the next scene. In short, there are numerous ways to join different scenes together. In this same way, conjunctions also join different grammatical elements together.

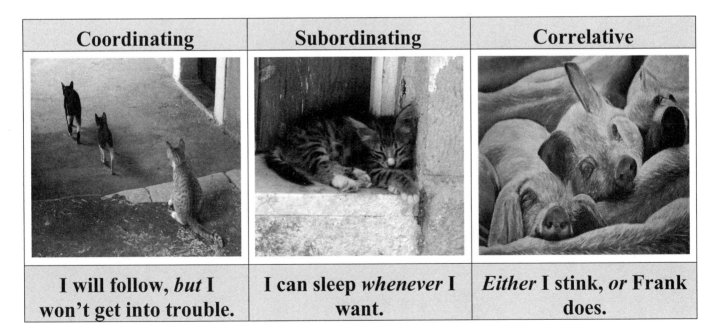

Coordinating	Subordinating	Correlative
I will follow, *but* I won't get into trouble.	I can sleep *whenever* I want.	*Either* I stink, *or* Frank does.

Travelogue

June 18th, 2006

Prophet Elijah's Church, Greece

The other day I had a really unique experience, **for** (coordinating conjunction) I went on an excursion to a small church. **Since** (subordinating conjunction) it was built on a deserted hill overlooking the sea, I had to drive for an hour through the White Mountains, named after their 9,000 foot peaks draped in a snow-colored dust. The church, dedicated to Prophet Elijah, required a strenuous hike **because** (subordinating conjunction) the deserted trail had long since been broken by winter rains; **not only** was the trail difficult to

navigate, **but** the wind was **also** (correlative conjunction) blowing ferociously with gusts over 50 mph. It was really difficult at times to walk up this hill **because** (subordinating conjunction) the wind was nearly buffeting me down the rocky slope. However, at the end of this adventurous hike, the view from the top was more than rewarding. **While** (subordinating conjunction) I stood surrounded by a panorama of cobalt sea, I could see the wind prick across the sea surface, picking up drops of moisture; it seemed like God breathing life into the sea. I stood in the wind **as** (subordinating conjunction) the few parishioners passed by into the church **so that** (subordinating conjunction) they honor Prophet Elijah's name day...

CONJUNCTION TYPES

Coordinating Conjunctions

These conjunctions join elements (words, phrases, clauses) of equal weight or function (they coordinate them).	**For, And, Nor, But, Or, Yet, So** To remember these conjunctions, think of the acronym they create: FANBOYS

- For this course, students will need scantrons **and** test-booklets.

The coordinating conjunction "and" joins the words/nouns "scantrons" and "booklets".

- When preparing for finals **and** working at the same time, students become exhausted.

The coordinating conjunction "and" joins the phrases "when preparing for finals" and "working at the same time".

- Instructors have to order books early in advance, **and** they also need to plan courses efficiently.

The coordinating conjunction "and" joins the clauses "Instructors…in advance" and "they also…efficiently."

Subordinating Conjunctions

These conjunctions join clauses of unequal weight or different function. In that way, they subordinate one clause to the other by creating dependence and a certain relationship (time, cause/effect, result, etc.) among the various clauses.	**Time**: after, before, once, since, until, when, whenever, while **Condition**: if, even if, provided that, unless **Contrast**: although, even though, though, whereas **Location**: wherever, where **Choice**: than, whether **Cause/Effect**: as, because, since **Result**: so that, in order that, that

- **After** the instructor explained the concept, the students had to write a paper on it.

The subordinating conjunction "after" joins the two clauses "the instructor…concept" and "the students…on it" and creates a relationship of time.

- **If** one studies diligently throughout the quarter, one does not have to worry about final exams.

The subordinating conjunction "if" joins the two clauses "one studies…quarter" and "one …exams" and creates a relationship of condition.

- **Although** students are mostly displeased with rising tuition fees, they still try to go through college.

The subordinating conjunction "although" joins the two clauses "students…fees" and "they…college" and creates a relationship of contrast.

Correlative Conjunctions

These conjunctions join elements of equal weight. Like coordinating conjunctions, they can join words, phrases, and clauses. However, these conjunctions are always paired for meaning and emphasis.

both…and, either…or, neither…nor, not only…but also

- For this course, students will need **both** scantrons **and** test-booklets.

The correlative conjunctions "both…and" join the words/nouns "scantrons" and "booklets".

- **Both** preparing for finals **and** working at the same time can make students exhausted.

The correlative conjunctions "both…and" join the phrases "preparing for finals" and "working at the same time".

- Instructors **not only** have to order books early in advance, **but** they **also** need to plan courses efficiently.

The correlative conjunctions "not only…but also" join the clauses "Instructors…in advance" and "they also…efficiently."

Highlight Points:
Conjunctions and Comma Usage
Comma usage can be tricky when using conjunctions. The following are some helpful rules to ensure correct comma usage. One can also consult the chapter on sentence structure.
A. Coordinating Conjunctions
➢ You **do need** a comma when the coordinating conjunction joins two independent clauses (for more see Sentence Structures: Sentence Types).
   *Administrators outline campus policies, **and** they help apply them.*
   The coordinating conjunction "and" joins the two independent clauses "Administrators…policies" and "they…them." A comma is necessary.
➢ You **do not need** a comma when the coordinating conjunction joins two elements other than Independent Clauses.
   Administrators outline campus policies and apply them.
   The coordinating conjunction "and" joins the elements (phrases) "outline campus policies" and "apply them". A comma is not necessary.
➢ You **do need** commas when the coordinating conjunction joins more than two elements together (usually in lists).
   *Administrators outline, implement, **and** assess campus policies.*
   The coordinating conjunction "and" joins the three verbs "outline", "implement", and "assess". Commas are necessary.

B. Subordinating Conjunctions

➢ You **do need** a comma when the clause introduced with a subordinating conjunction (dependent clause) precedes an independent clause.

> *If students come to class late, they might miss a quiz.*

➢ You **do not need** a comma when the clause introduced with a subordinating conjunction (dependent clause) follows an independent clause.

> *Students might miss a quiz if they come to class late.*

C. Correlative Conjunctions

Correlative conjunctions follow the same rules as coordinating conjunctions, for their second component is a coordinating conjunction (both…**and**, not only…**but** also, neither…**nor**, either…**or**).

Broadening One's Horizons

Real traveling should open our minds to alternative lifestyles **and** modes of thought, but this doesn't mean that we should entirely abandon our own values or system of doing things when we encounter other lands, people, and cultures. It doesn't mean, for instance, that if in one culture horse meat is considered a delicacy we should sit down to a feast of stallions. In Italy, horse meat is regularly eaten while in California it was made illegal by proposition. Travel to Italy entails neither that we should feast on horses nor that we immediately condemn Italians as barbarians for doing so. Real traveling can be conducive not only to photo albums and souvenir collections but also to education. We can see it as an opportunity to reevaluate our own cultural preconceptions so that we understand if not appreciate the culture, the people, and the places we visit. Indeed, what we initially see may have little connection to the reality of the place we are visiting.

Practice with Conjunctions

1. Identify all the conjunctions in the text by underlining them. Then, find the words or groups of words these conjunctions join— *e.g. and: it joins the words "lifestyles/modes"*.

2. Label each underlined conjunction according to its type (coordinating, subordinating, correlative etc.)— *e.g. and: coordinating conjunction.*

3. In the paragraph you have constructed about your classroom, try to identify all the conjunctions you have used and then try to add more conjunctions to further join the elements in your paragraph. Last, try to apply exercises 1-2 to your paragraph.

Ancient *and* Modern

Coordinating Conjunction

Neither Wood *nor* Bear

Correlative Conjunction

Chapter One--Mini-Review: Conjunctions

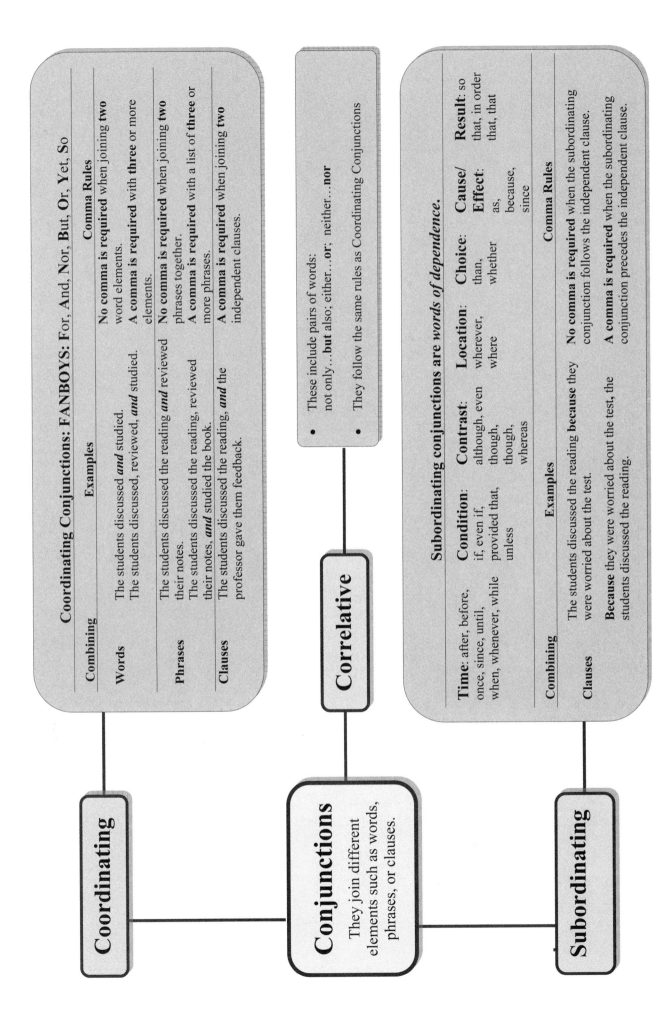

Conjunctions

They join different elements such as words, phrases, or clauses.

Coordinating

Coordinating Conjunctions: FANBOYS: For, And, Nor, But, Or, Yet, So

Combining	Examples	Comma Rules
Words	The students discussed *and* studied.	No comma is required when joining two word elements.
	The students discussed, reviewed, *and* studied.	A comma is required with **three** or more elements.
Phrases	The students discussed the reading *and* reviewed their notes.	No comma is required when joining **two** phrases together.
	The students discussed the reading, reviewed their notes, *and* studied the book.	A comma is required with a list of **three** or more phrases.
Clauses	The students discussed the reading, *and* the professor gave them feedback.	A comma is required when joining **two** independent clauses.

Correlative

- These include pairs of words: not only...**but** also; either...**or**; neither...**nor**
- They follow the same rules as Coordinating Conjunctions

Subordinating

Subordinating conjunctions are *words of dependence.*

Time: after, before, once, since, until, when, whenever, while	**Condition:** if, even if, provided that, unless	**Contrast:** although, even though, though, whereas	**Location:** wherever, where	**Choice:** than, whether	**Cause/ Effect:** as, because, since	**Result:** so that, in order that, that

Combining	Examples	Comma Rules
Clauses	The students discussed the reading **because** they were worried about the test.	**No comma is required** when the subordinating conjunction follows the independent clause.
	Because they were worried about the test, the students discussed the reading.	**A comma is required** when the subordinating conjunction precedes the independent clause.

PREPOSITIONS

Formal Definition

<u>Form</u>: Prepositions, which may consist of one or more words, may take an object. The group of words formed by the preposition and its object is called a "prepositional phrase", and it conveys information about time, manner, and place (for more see Sentence Structures: Phrases).

Prepositions may also accompany verbs, forming Phrasal Verbs (idiomatic verbs that require specific prepositions). (

<u>Function</u>: In a sentence, a prepositional phrase or a preposition is used to modify other elements of the sentence. If it is used to modify a noun or a pronoun, it functions as an adjective. If it is used to modify a verb, adverb, or a clause, it functions as an adverb or helps create a phrasal verb.

<u>Etymology</u>: The word *preposition* derives from the Latin words *pre + positus*, meaning *before + position*. This is exactly what prepositions do: they are positioned in front of their object to show its relationship to other elements in the sentence.

Informal Definition

Once a film has been completed, the director and editor must sign off. Then, the film is placed in the hands of the marketers. It is they who decide during which time the film is to be released, within what audience demographic, and in what way the trailer is to be presented. In this same way, prepositions form groups of words that modify other elements in a clause or a sentence.

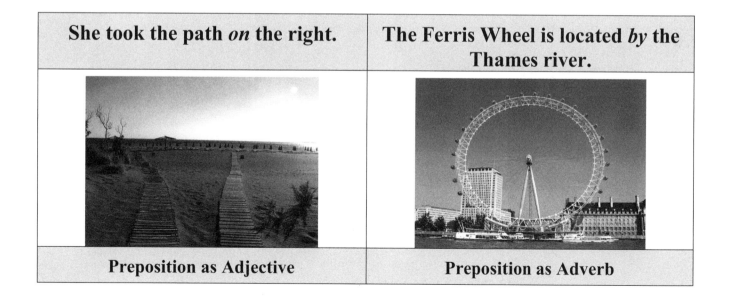

She took the path *on* the right.	The Ferris Wheel is located *by* the Thames river.
Preposition as Adjective	Preposition as Adverb

Travelogue

June 19th, 2006

Mike's Coffee Shop, Greece

The village of *Vrisses* seemed deserted **upon** my arrival, but it was really just **during** siesta time. **After** 6:30 in the evening, all the villagers came **out** to sit **on** their verandas or **at** the *Kaffenio* (local coffee shop). This *Kaffenio* was owned **by** an ancient Greek-American named Mike, who greeted me **by** saying, "I have the best Greek coffee **in** the world. I mean the best. Take a seat." What could I do but accept a seat **from** a man dressed **in** traditional Cretan attire and

test **out** his assertion? Mike's *Kaffenio* attracts all the old folks **from** the village, who sit **for** hours **on** stiff wooden chairs, hunched **over** their small cups **of** coffee and boards **of** backgammon, talking **about** life, politics, and the world. Mike was one **of** those interesting characters you rarely meet, for he had spent 30 years or so **in** New York and had returned **to** *Vrisses* **in** 1994. **At** one point, Mike took me aside and told me that we could make a lot **of** money together. He was thinking **about** converting his *Kaffenio* **into** a *taverna* (small local restaurant) and just needed money, a cook, a waiter, and a manager. His cousin would serve customers, his wife would cook, and I would provide the money necessary and then manage everything. It was unclear what Mike would do, but I'm sure he had a plan **about** that too. If this cunning plan failed to work, Mike said, we could then go **into** the olive oil production business together! Either I inspired a great deal **of** trust **in** Mike, or his coffee was too potent.

Preposition as Adjective

Prepositional Phrases as Adjectives: when they modify a noun or a pronoun.

The tall Bell Tower *in the quad* is a symbol *of the University*.

The prepositional phrase "in the quad" modifies the noun "Tower", and the prepositional phrase "of the University" modifies the noun "symbol". Therefore, these prepositional phrases function as adjectives.

Preposition as Adverb

Prepositional Phrases as Adverbs: when they modify a verb, an adverb, an adjective, or a clause.

The tall Bell Tower is found *in the center* of campus.

The prepositional phrase "in the center" modifies the verb "is found" and functions as an adverb that shows location.

Preposition as Part of Phrasal Verb

Prepositions as part of Phrasal Verbs: when they are paired with idiomatic verbs.

Transitive Phrasal Verbs: these phrasal verbs take an object with their preposition, and they come in two types:

> **Separable**: *these transitive phrasal verbs can either have their object after the preposition or before.*

> > The instructor **brought** *up* many interesting issues. **OR**

> > The instructor **brought** many interesting issues *up*.

> **Inseparable**: *these transitive phrasal verbs can have their object only after the preposition.*

> > Good instructors **look** *after* their students. **NOT**

> > ~~Good instructors look their students after~~.

Intransitive Phrasal Verbs: these phrasal verbs do not take an object after their preposition.

> Students tend to miss morning classes because they **sleep** *in*.

Common Phrasal Verbs

add up *(add)*

break down *(analyze)*

bring up *(raise)*

call up *(telephone)*

carry on *(continue)*

count in *(include)*

dress up *(put clothes on)*

eat up *(eat completely)*

figure out *(interpret)*

fill out *(complete)*

find out *(discover)*

fix up *(repair)*

give up *(surrender)*

give away *(distribute)*

hand over *(yield control)*

hold up *(delay)*

keep up *(continue)*

leave out *(omit)*

let down *(disappoint)*

light up *(light)*

make over *(remake)*

pass out *(distribute)*

play down *(minimize)*

point out *(indicate)*

put off *(postpone)*

put up *(host a guest)*

quiet down (quiet)

ring up *(telephone)*

rule out *(eliminate)*

run off *(cause to depart)*

save up *(accumulate)*

set up *(arrange)*

show off *(exhibit proudly)*

shut off *(cease functioning)*

spell out *(state in detail)*

take back *(return)*

take over *(assume command)*

tear down *(destroy)*

think over *(consider)*

throw away *(discard)*

tire out *(become exhausted)*

turn down *(refuse)*

turn out *(produce)*

wash off *(wash)*

wear out *(use until unusable)*

wipe out *(decimate)*

work out *(solve)*

write up *(compose a document)*

Common Prepositions

about	by	on
above	down	over
across	during	since
after	except	through
along	from	to
among	in	toward
apart from	in addition to	under
as	in front of	until
at	in place of	up
because of	including	upon
before	inside	via
behind	instead of	with
below	into	with reference to
beside	like	with respect to
between	near	within
beyond	of	without

Highlight Points:

Prepositions vs. Conjunctions

Prepositions should not be confused with conjunctions. Although some prepositions have the same form as some conjunctions, they function differently. Therefore, despite the same form, one needs to look at the function of the word within the specific sentence to determine what part of speech the word belongs to.

- *The instructor placed the book on reserve **for** the students. (**Preposition**)*

  The word "for" in this sentence is a preposition followed by its object "students". This prepositional phrase, then, functions as an adjective that modifies the noun "book".

- *The instructor placed the book on reserve, **for** some students could not find it at the bookstore. (**Coordinating Conjunction**)*

  The word "for" in this sentence is a coordinating conjunction because it joins two clauses of equal weight, "The instructor...reserve" and "some students...bookstore".

Educational Adventures

Wide exposure **to** many of the world's cultures through travel stimulates our critical faculties. We are more likely to evaluate why we do the things we do as well as to ascertain what preconceptions for behavior and demeanor we all have. Likewise, in the next encounter when someone appears ill-mannered, we might pause a second or two to consider the possible reasons for this before condemning him as one of "those people". Finally, while travel is no panacea for the world's ills, understanding through exposure to other cultures might prove to be an educational adventure as well as a way to strengthen bonds among the world's peoples.

Practice with Prepositions

1. Identify all the prepositions in the text by underlining them. Then, find the words these prepositions accompany (prepositional phrases or phrasal verbs)— *e.g. (exposure) to: accompanies "many of the world's cultures".*

2. Label each underlined preposition according to its type (as adjectives, as adverbs, as part of phrasal verb)— *e.g. (exposure) to: as an adjective.*

3. In the paragraph you have constructed about your classroom try to identify all the prepositions you have used and then try to apply exercises 1-2 to your paragraph.

The Golden Gate stretches *over* the Bay.

Preposition Modifying a Verb (as Adverb)

A Tea House *in* China

Preposition Modifying a Noun (as Adjective)

Chapter One--Mini-Review: Prepositions

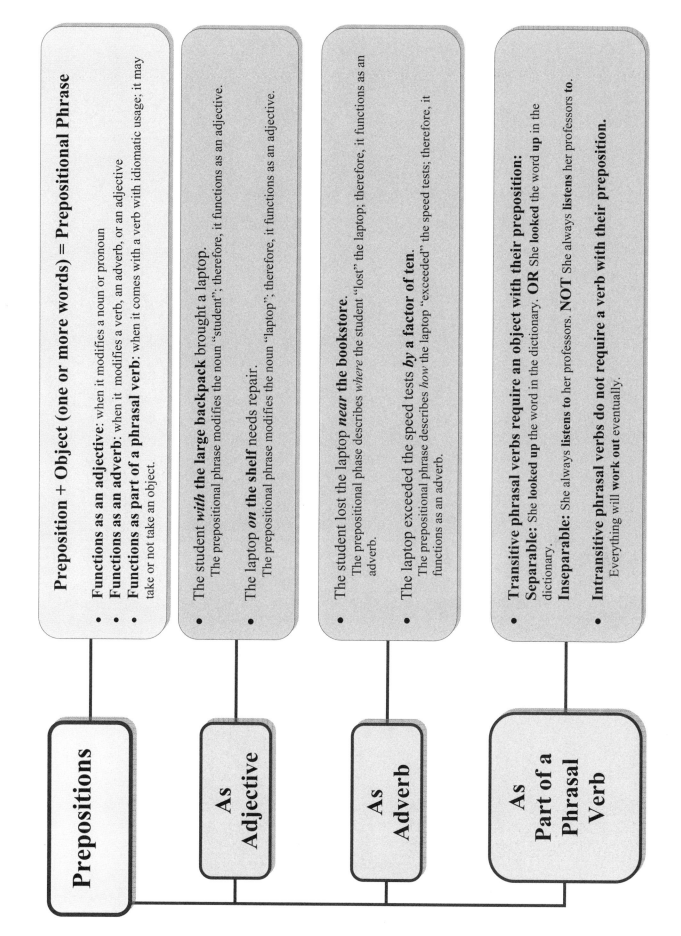

Prepositions

Preposition + Object (one or more words) = Prepositional Phrase

- **Functions as an adjective:** when it modifies a noun or pronoun
- **Functions as an adverb:** when it modifies a verb, an adverb, or an adjective
- **Functions as part of a phrasal verb:** when it comes with a verb with idiomatic usage; it may take or not take an object.

As Adjective

- The student *with the large backpack* brought a laptop.
  The prepositional phrase modifies the noun "student"; therefore, it functions as an adjective.
- The laptop *on the shelf* needs repair.
  The prepositional phrase modifies the noun "laptop"; therefore, it functions as an adjective.

As Adverb

- The student lost the laptop *near the bookstore.*
  The prepositional phrase describes *where* the student "lost" the laptop; therefore, it functions as an adverb.
- The laptop exceeded the speed tests *by a factor of ten.*
  The prepositional phrase describes *how* the laptop "exceeded" the speed tests; therefore, it functions as an adverb.

As Part of a Phrasal Verb

- **Transitive phrasal verbs require an object with their preposition:**
  Separable: She looked **up** the word in the dictionary. **OR** She looked the word **up** in the dictionary.
  Inseparable: She always **listens** her professors. **NOT** She always **listens** her professors **to**.
- **Intransitive phrasal verbs do not require a verb with their preposition.**
  Everything will work out eventually.

INTERJECTIONS

INTERJECTION DEFINITIONS

Formal Definition

Form: Interjections are words that convey emphasis, surprise, or strong emotion. They are usually punctuated by an exclamation point (!) or within commas.

Function: These words are used for emphasis and are not often found in academic writing unless they appear in quotes. They usually have no grammatical connection to the rest of the sentence.

Etymology: The word *interjection* derives from the Latin words *inter* + iacere, meaning *between* + *to throw*. This is exactly how interjections function: they are "thrown" between or among other words or sentences for emphasis.

Informal Definition

Once a film actually reaches an audience, the director and the whole film team look to the audience for their reactions. If the audience exits the cinema and they have only one-word exclamations (hopefully good ones), then the film team knows that they succeeded. These spontaneous responses that include words like "woe", "wow", and "hey" can be good indicators for the enjoyment and potential success of the film. Likewise, if audience members leave and the only thing they have to say is "uggh" or "aaghh," then the film is not long for the screen. In this same way, interjections function to emphasize some kind of feeling or reaction.

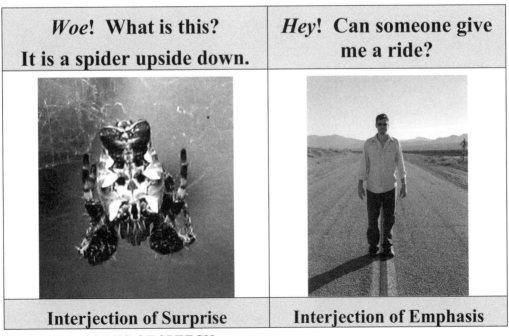

Woe! What is this? It is a spider upside down.	*Hey*! Can someone give me a ride?
Interjection of Surprise	Interjection of Emphasis

Travelogue

June 21st, 2006
The Man from Uruguay

During one of my day trips in Greece, I met this guy from Uruguay. We went sightseeing together, and at one point he told me this joke they have in his country about Americans: "There's this fisherman on a perfect beach down in Uruguay with a small bucket of fish next to him. An American, who has been watching the fisherman for some time, approaches him and says, 'Hey, that's some nice looking fish you have there. How long have you been here for?' 'Um, since 10:00 this morning' the fisherman replied. 'Aha!' said the American, 'You know, if

you were to get up just a little bit earlier, you could catch even more fish and fill up the bucket.' The Uruguayan, seeming skeptical, questioned, 'Hmm, why should I do that?' The American thought for a moment, 'Well, you could sell the surplus and then maybe in a few years even buy a boat with some nets.' The Uruguayan looked puzzled, 'Aha!! I see, but why would I want to do that?' The American looked a bit exasperated, 'Pfff, well, if you bought a boat, you could catch 10 times more fish, and in a couple years you could even buy a whole fleet of boats.' The Uruguayan's eyebrow went up, 'Ok, why would I want to do that?' The American was nearly excited now by the idea, 'Well, then you could have an ample retirement, play cards with your friends, and drink beer all day.' The Uruguayan grabbed his bucket and his pole and began to walk away. 'Hey, where are you going now?' the American asked. The Uruguayan smiled, 'I am going home to play cards with my friends and drink beer for the rest of the day. Cheers!'"

Chapter 2
Verb Tenses

If parts of speech are the building blocks of language, then verbs are the foundation of this building. For this foundation to be solid, verbs need to be used in the correct tense. In English, there are twelve distinct verb tenses:

Past Tenses	**Simple Past, Past Progressive, Past Perfect, Past Perfect Progressive**
Present Tenses	**Simple Present, Present Progressive, Present Perfect, Present Perfect Progressive**
Future Tenses	**Simple Future, Future Progressive, Future Perfect, Future Perfect Progressive**

Verb tenses are necessary in order to understand time; they enable us to distinguish the past from the present and the future. They help us remember the past, live in the present, and plan for the future. To construct language correctly, one needs to be familiar with both the form and the function of these verb tenses as well as to follow certain rules about their usage; otherwise, if one uses these verb tenses incorrectly, one might be lost in time.

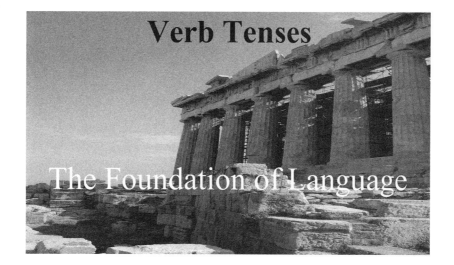

VERB TENSES

Formal Definition

<u>Form</u>: Verb tenses are the various forms verbs adopt in order to convey information about the time of an action, occurrence, or state of being. In English, there are twelve distinct verb tenses. These verb tenses change their form according to the specific **time dimension** and **time circumstances** they express.

<u>Function</u>: Verb tenses convey information about a specific **time dimension** (past, present, or future) and about specific **time circumstances** such as repetition, in-progress, perfection, and continuation/duration (tense types: simple, progressive, perfect, perfect progressive). The choice of a specific verb tense is very important because it positions the action, occurrence, or state of being of the verb in time.

<u>Etymology</u>: The word *tense* derives from the Latin word *tempus*, meaning *time*. This is exactly what verb tenses do: they position any action, occurrence, or state of being in time.

Informal Definition

Imagine you want to travel in time with your brand new time machine. Where would you go? First of all, you need to decide whether to travel into the past, stay in the present, or transfer into the future (Time Dimension). So, let's say you want to go back in time to President Lincoln and the Gettysburg Address, November 19th, 1863. Do you want to 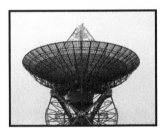 *arrive when he is in the process of giving the speech (in-progress) or after he has completed the speech (perfection)? Therefore, besides the time dimension, you also need to tell your time machine what specific time circumstances you want to arrive in. In English, verb tenses are your time machine.*

Past	Present	Future
I *survived* World War II.	I *work* as a teacher.	I *will be* a real thinker one day.

TIME DIMENSIONS

Verb tenses are classified into three distinct **time dimensions**: **past**, **present**, and **future**. It is important to realize that although these time dimensions seem obvious, many languages do not express them through different verb forms (verb tenses). Other languages such as Chinese convey information about time through adverbs. English, on the contrary, does shape verbs in such a way that they themselves can express time on their own without needing other words like adverbs.

> Chinese (translated):
>
> Many international students **attend** courses in American universities **last year**.
>
> *In Chinese, it is not the verb "attend" that conveys information about the time of the action (when students attend courses?); it is the adverbial phrase "last year" that does.*
>
> English:
>
> Many international students **attended** courses in American universities (last year).
>
> *In English, it is the verb "attend" through its Simple Past Tense (--ed) Form (attend-ed) that conveys information about the time of the action (past); the adverb "last year" is optional.*

Knowing or deciding when an action, occurrence, or state of being happens or exists is the **first most important step** in choosing the correct verb tense: therefore, one first needs to position the verb (action, occurrence, state of being) in one of these dimensions: **past**, **present**, or **future**.

TIME CIRCUMSTANCES

Besides a specific time dimension, verb tenses also convey more specific information about the time of an action, occurrence, or state of being. If one, for instance, knows that the action happened in the past, the present, or the future, then one also may need to know whether the action was repeated, in-progress, perfected, or whether and for how long it has been going on. Therefore, besides the time dimension, verb tenses also express specific circumstances about time: repetition, in-progress, perfection, continuation/duration. After you determine the time dimension (past, present, future) of an action, occurrence, or state of being, knowing or deciding their specific time circumstances is **the second most important step** in choosing the correct verb tense.

> Chinese (translated):
>
> Many international students **attend** courses in American universities **for the entire next year**.
>
> *In Chinese, it is not the verb "attend" that conveys information about the time of the action (when students attend courses?); it is the prepositional phrase "for the entire next year" that does. This phrase does not only show a time dimension (future) but also the specific time circumstances of the action (in-progress).*

English:

Many international students **will be attending** courses in American universities (for the entire next year).

In English, it is the verb "attend" through its Future Progressive Tense (will be attending) that conveys information not only about the time dimension of the action (future) but also about the time circumstances of the action (in-progress). Therefore, the verb tense "will be attending" informs us that the action of "attending" will be in progress for a certain period of time in the future.

In conclusion, it is the time dimensions (past, present, future) in combination with the time circumstances (repetition, in-progress, perfection (by), continuation /duration) that determine the specific verb tense that should be used. **In deciding, then, which verb tense is appropriate, one needs to first determine the time dimension and second the time circumstance of the action, occurrence, or state of being.**

Verb tenses are classified into four different types according to the different time circumstances they express: **Simple**, **Progressive**, **Perfect**, **Perfect Progressive**.

Travelogue

June 21st, 2006

The Stone Village of Koumos, Greece

A trip to Greece **is** (Present/Repetition-Truth) not only about visiting big cities and seeing museums. It **is** (Present/Repetition-Truth) also about journeying out to the countryside to see villages that **have populated** (Present/Perfection (by)) the landscape for hundreds of years. In one of these villages, I **came** (Past/Completion) across a native rock artist who **had been laboring** (Past/Continuation) on a series of stone buildings for many years. With stones and rocks he **gathered** (Past/Completion) from the neighboring countryside, he **built** (Past/Completion) a small church, a house, a barn, a battlement (complete with a canon), and few guest rooms. The artist, Georgos Halevelakis, **is** (Present/Repetition/Truth) old enough to retire; however, he **is** (Present/Repetition) still dedicated to his art and fascinated by the forces nature **exerts** (Present/Truth) on the stones around him. He **has been gathering** (Present/Continuation) the most interesting and expressive rocks and stones and **has been laying** (Present/Continuation) them with great skill and artistry for over twenty years now. Actually, he **has** (Present/Repetition) no plans to stop.

What **is** (Present/Repetition) really remarkable about his stone creations **is** (Present/Truth) that he **does not alter** (Present/Repetition) the stones or the rocks in any way. Instead, he **retains** (Present/Repetition) the shapes and textures of each and every rock, and with great patience he **finds** (Present/Repetition) ways to combine these stones into a series of creations that **blend** (Present/Repetition) harmoniously with the environment and **allow** (Present/Repetition) the stones to express their geological history. With little help, Georgos Halevelakis **lets** (Present/Repetition) the stones tell their own stories. I **hope** (Present/Repetition) he **will be** (Future/Repetition) able to express his creativity for another twenty years!

Simple Tenses
Repetition/ (Completion)

Simple Past	Simple Present	Simple Future
I studied.	I study.	I will study.

Time Circumstances: **Simple** Tenses indicate that the action, occurrence, or state of being of the verb is consistently true, habitual, or relevant to a particular moment in time. With these tenses, then the emphasis is **usually** on the **repetition** of the action in time.

Progressive Tenses
In-Progress

Past Progressive	Present Progressive	Future Progressive
I was studying.	I am studying.	I will be studying.

Time Circumstances: **Progressive** Tenses indicate that the action, occurrence, state of being of the verb is ongoing, **in-progress** in the past, present, or future. With these tenses, then, the **emphasis** is on the ongoing, **in-progress** effect of the action, occurrence, or state of being.

Perfect Tenses
Perfection by a certain point in time

Past Perfect	Present Perfect	Future Perfect
I had studied.	I have studied.	I will have studied.

Time Circumstances: **Perfect** Tenses indicate that the action, occurrence, or state of being of the verb has been **perfected** by a certain point in the past, present, or future. With these tenses, then, the **emphasis** is on the **perfection** of the action **by a certain point in time**. Perfection here means ending, finish and not the state of being perfect, immaculate.

Perfect Progressive Tenses
Continuation/Duration

Past Perfect Progressive	Present Perfect Progressive	Future Perfect Progressive
I had been studying.	I have been studying.	I will have been studying.

Time Circumstances: **Perfect Progressive** Tenses indicate that the action, occurrence, or state of being of the verb started **at a certain point** in the past but is **not perfected** yet; it was/is/will be still **in-progress**. With these tenses, then, the **emphasis** is on the **continuation/duration** of the action **between two distinct points in time**. Therefore, these tenses combine the time circumstances of perfect and progressive tenses.

Highlight Points:
Time Indicators
A. In English, it is not only verb tenses that convey information about time. All of the following parts of speech can also express time. What is important to realize is that the verb **has to** express time; even if you have other time indicators, they cannot substitute for the correct verb tense.

- Verb Tenses:
    *All students **turned in** their journals.*
    Here, the verb "turned in" in the Simple Past Tense (--ed) Form conveys information about the time dimension (past) and circumstance (repetition/completion) of the action.

- Adverbs:
    *All students **turned in** their journals **weekly**.*
    Here, besides the verb "turned in", the adverb "weekly" also conveys information about the frequency of the action in the past.

- Adjectives:
    *All students **turned in** their **weekly** journals.*
    Here, besides the verb "turned in", the adjective "weekly", by modifying the noun "journals", also conveys information about the frequency of the action in the past.

- Prepositional Phrases:
    *All students **turned in** their journals **at the end of every week**.*
    Here, besides the verb "turned in", the prepositional phrase "at the end of every week", by modifying the verb "turned in", conveys information about the frequency of the action.

- Conjunctions (introducing time clauses):
    ***When** each week ended, students **turned in** their journals.*
    Here, the subordinating conjunction "when" and the clause it introduces "each week ended", by modifying the verb "turned in", convey information about the frequency of the action.

B. All of the above time indicators, when combined, have to be compatible in terms of time dimension and time circumstances.

> *All students **turned in** their journals **tomorrow**.*
> *Here, the verb "turned in" conveys information about a time dimension (past) different from the time dimension expressed through the adverb "tomorrow" (future).*

Progressive Tenses and State of Being Verbs

In English, the verbs that show the subject's state of being usually do not form the progressive tenses.

- Mental State: believe, desire, imagine, know, ***forget***, realize, ***remember***, ***think***
- Emotional State: appreciate, dislike, feel, fear, like, love, please, prefer, etc.
- Ownership State: belong, ***have***, own, etc.
- Sensory State: hear, feel, smell, see, sound, taste
- Other: appear, be, contain, exist, ***look***, look like, resemble, seem, etc.

The verbs in bold and italics can occasionally form progressive tenses in case they function as transitive verbs with an object.

*This exam **looks** perfect. I **am looking** at it right now.*

Working with One's Hands

My father is a medical doctor and currently 70 years old but still greatly enjoys harvesting olives despite everyone's objections. When he **was** younger, he actually enjoyed how at various social gatherings his colleagues and other intellectuals were feeling awkward or condescending when they listened to his agricultural endeavors. They were probably thinking at that time that my father was short of money because he had degraded himself to the level of a manual worker. To this day in many societies, manual labor has had the pejorative connotation of a lesser form of work, something that has never been equal in some important way to the intellectual efforts of doctors, computer specialists, or any white collar type of job. Indeed, many people think manual work is the hard road to be traveled by people without any education, real skills, or alternatives. Many people disregard manual labor as inferior, and monetarily, intellectually, and emotionally less fulfilling than the more intellectual endeavors of other jobs. However, this is not further from the truth. Those who work with their hands will often experience a deep sense of satisfaction about their work equal or even greater to those that work with their minds.

Practice with Time

1. Identify all the verbs in the text by underlining them.

2. Make three separate columns: a) list all verbs in the past--*e.g. was*; b) list all verbs in the present; c) list all verbs in the future.

3. Next to each verb in the chart you have assembled, write the specific time circumstance of the verb (repetition/ (completion), in-progress, perfection, continuation/duration).

4. Next to each verb in the chart you have assembled, write the specific tense the verb is in (Past Perfect, Present Perfect, etc.).

Mountainous Villages

Life in the village *is* hard but also interesting.
Time Dimension: Present/ Time Circumstance:
Repitition/ Verb Tense: Simple Present

PRESENT TENSES

Simple Present Tense
Time Dimension: Present; Time Circumstance: Repetition

Form	Base Form of the verb **Or** (-s) Form of the verb only for the Third Person Singular

Function	➢ Habitual action, occurrence, or state of being in the present
	
	      Every student usually **works** hard during finals' week. *(-s Form)*
	
	      Students consistently **work** hard during finals' week. *(Base Form)*
	
	 ➢ Consistently true action, occurrence, or state of being
	
	      The earth **revolves** around the sun.
	
	 ➢ Discussion of literature and film
	
	      According to Shakespeare, Macbeth **suffers** for murdering his king.

Highlight Points:
Attention for the Positive, Negative, and Interrogative Forms of the Simple Present
➢ Positive Form:
Form: Auxiliary Verb (to do) in the Simple Present Tense + Base Form of the verb
I do, you do, he/she/it does, we/you/they do
Function: This form is only used for emphasis.
     *You are wrong. Maria **does study** hard all the time!*
     Here, by using the auxiliary verb "to do", there is an emphasis on the truth of the statement.
➢ Negative Form:
Form: Auxiliary Verb (to do) in the Simple Present Tense + Base Form of the verb
I do not (don't), you do not (don't), he/she/it does (doesn't), we/you/they do not (don't)
Function: This is the form used in negative statements.
     *Maria **does not (doesn't) study** hard all the time.*
➢ Interrogative Form:
Form: Auxiliary Verb (to do) in the Simple Present Tense + Base Form of the verb
I do not (don't), you do not (don't), he/she/it does (doesn't), we/you/they do not (don't)
Function: This is the form used in questions and in inverted word order.
     ***Does** Maria **study** hard all the time?*

Present Progressive Tense
Time Dimension: Present; Time Circumstance: In-Progress

Form	Auxiliary Verb (to be) in the Simple Present Tense *I am, you are, he/she/it is, we/you/they are* + Present Participle (-ing) Form of the verb
Function	➤ Action, occurrence, state of being that is **in-progress in the present** Students **are working** on a grammar exercise in class right now. She **is working** on her dissertation. *Here, the emphasis is on the in-progress effect of the action in the present.*

Highlight Points:

A. The "Going to" Form

Form: Auxiliary Verb (to be) + Present Progressive Tense of the verb (to go) + Infinitive Form (to) of the verb

I am going, you are going, he/she/it is going, we/you/they are going

Function: Although this is a verb in the Present Progressive Tense, the whole phrase is idiomatic and describes action, occurrence, or state of being in the future.

*I **am going to study** for my finals tomorrow.*

*We **are not going to graduate** at the end of this year if we don't study hard.*

B. Stative Verbs

Some English verbs have stative meanings (describing states, conditions, or situations). These stative verbs usually do not form the progressive tenses (Present Progressive, Past Progressive, etc.) For more on these verbs, see the chart at the end of the chapter.

	Present Perfect Tense
	Time Dimension: Present; Time Circumstance: Perfection

	Auxiliary Verb (to have) in the Simple Present Tense
	I have, you have, he/she/it has, we/you/they have
Form	+
	Past Participle (--ed) Form of the verb

	➢ Action, occurrence, or state of being that began in the past and is **perfected by some point in the present**
	Students **have worked** on a grammar exercise today.
Function	She **has finished her dissertation** (by now).
	Here, the emphasis is on the perfection of the action by some point in the present. The point in the present sometimes is explicitly described (example #1: "today"), and sometimes it is only implicitly described (example#2: "by now" is implied.)

	Present Perfect Progressive Tense
	Time Dimension: Present; Time Circumstance: Continuation/Duration

	Auxiliary Verb (to be) in the Present Perfect Tense
	I have been, you have been, he/she/it has been, we/you/they have been
Form	+
	Present Participle (--ing) Form of the verb

	➢ Action, occurrence, or state of being that started at a certain point in the past but has **not** been **perfected** yet; it is still **in-progress in the present**.
	Students **have been working** on a grammar exercise today.
Function	Marisa **has been working** on her dissertation for the last five years.
	Here, the emphasis is on the continuation/duration of the action between two distinct points in time. The action started at some point in the past and is still lasting in the present. Actually, it is still in-progress in the present.

Highlight Points:

Present Perfect Tense vs. Present Perfect Progressive Tense

What is the real difference? These two tenses might be confusing sometimes, but following the rules about the time dimension and time circumstances of the action, occurrence, or state of being of the verb can solve possible problems.

➤ <u>Present Perfect Tense:</u>

*Students **have worked** on a grammar exercise today.*

*Here, the action started in the past and has been perfected by a certain point in the present. The emphasis, then, is on the **perfection** of the action **by a certain point in the present**. Actually, the verb tense informs us that the students have finished a grammar exercise **today**.*

➤ <u>Present Perfect Progressive Tense:</u>

*Students **have been working** on a grammar exercise today.*

*Here, the emphasis is on the **continuation/duration** of the action between two distinct points in time. The action started at some point in the past and is still going on in the present. Actually, the verb tense informs us that the students started working on a grammar exercise in the past and are still working on it in the present.*

Travelogue

June 22nd, 2006
The Village of Louhi, Greece

Lyrics from an old Cretan song **claim** (Simple Present) that Crete **is** (Simple Present) not an island; it **is** (Simple Present) a beast that lays itself on the sea because of the wildness of its nature and the strength of its people. Indeed, journeying through the Cretan countryside, one **comes** (Simple Present) across villages and people that time **has**

passed by (Present Perfect) without substantially altering. One such place **is** (Simple Present) Louhi, a village which **is** (Simple Present) situated in a mountainous area in Western Crete. Its population **has** significantly **diminished** (Present Perfect) since the 1960s, and it now **hosts** a meager ten inhabitants who proudly **name** it their home. Louhi **is** (Simple Present) not for the young or the faint of heart, for the average age of its residents **is** (Simple Present) seventy. Even so, these seventy-year olds, who **have spent** almost their entire lives here, **are** (Simple Present) still strong and healthy; it **is** amazing to observe them while they **are cutting** (Present Progressive) wood, **milking** goats, **harvesting** (Present Progressive) olives and grapes, and **making** (Present Progressive) their own wine. It **is** (Simple Present) probably the hard work, the clean air, and the fresh food that **have been breeding** (Present Perfect Progressive) such tenacity and endurance. It **is** (Simple Present) not, however, just the people that **grow** (Simple Present) strong and old. Even squash **does** (Simple Present)!

Manual Labor

Manual work **is** never really "unskilled" or "mindless". Quite the contrary, it exercises both the body and the mind, something that is not true for most intellectual jobs. To harvest olives, for instance, one needs to know the right time of year and to plan ahead. Furthermore, after one has secured the right tools and equipment, one needs to use these tools efficiently to avoid damaging the trees or hurting oneself. In addition, in today's era, almost no manual work is separate from science and technology. Indeed, for a long time many modern farmers, for instance, have been attending college or have already graduated from college with a theoretical and practical understanding of terms like "soil", "nutrients", and "fertilizers". Therefore, while the word manual derives from the Latin word "manus", meaning "hand", it does not entail that the mind remains passive in the whole process. Quite the contrary, manual work offers a balance between the mind and the body, a balance that intellectuals often seek while they are running on the treadmill of a gym's artificial environment.

Hand Washed Clothes

People **wash** clothes by hand.
Simple Present Tense/
Habitual Action

Practice with the Present

1. Identify all the verbs in the text by underlining them.

2. Make four separate columns: a) list all verbs in the Simple Present—*e.g. is*; b) list all verbs in the Present Progressive; c) list all verbs in the Present Perfect; d) list all verbs in the Present Perfect Progressive.

3. Next to each verb in the chart you have assembled, convert the present verb form into its past and future equivalents. Make sure to retain the same number and person of the verb—*e.g. (Manual work) is (Simple Present); was (Simple Past); will be (Simple Future).*

4. Choose one of your personal favorite pictures and write a story about it as if it were happening in the present. Be sure to include details of who, what, when, where, how, and why. Try to use as many present verb tenses as you can correctly.

Goat Crossing

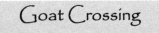

The goats **are escaping**!
Present Progressive Tense/
In-progress

PAST TENSES

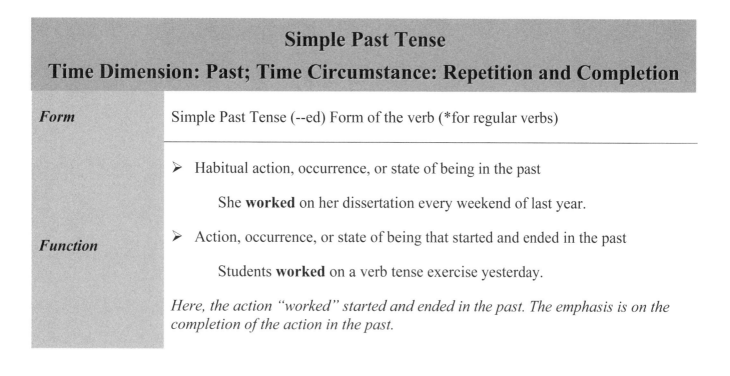

Simple Past Tense

Time Dimension: Past; Time Circumstance: Repetition and Completion

Form	Simple Past Tense (--ed) Form of the verb (*for regular verbs)
Function	➤ Habitual action, occurrence, or state of being in the past
	She **worked** on her dissertation every weekend of last year.
	➤ Action, occurrence, or state of being that started and ended in the past
	Students **worked** on a verb tense exercise yesterday.
	Here, the action "worked" started and ended in the past. The emphasis is on the completion of the action in the past.

Highlight Points:

Simple Past Tense vs. Present Perfect Tense

What is the real difference? These two tenses might be confusing sometimes, but following the rules about the time dimension and time circumstances of the action, occurrence, or state of being of the verb can solve possible problems.

➤ Simple Past Tense:

 Students **worked** *on a grammar exercise (yesterday).*

Here, the emphasis is on the completion of the action in the past. The action started at some point in the past and was completed in the past. Actually, the verb tense informs us that the students worked on a grammar exercise yesterday.

➤ Present Perfect Tense:

Students **have worked** *on a grammar exercise (by today).*

Here, the action started in the past and has been perfected by a certain point in the present. The emphasis, then, is on the **perfection** *of the action* **by a certain point in the present (today)**. *Actually, the verb tense informs us that the students have finished a grammar exercise today (by the time we make this statement).*

Could we say: Students **have worked** *on a grammar exercise yesterday?*

No, because the present perfect indicates that the perfection of the action happened by a certain point in the present and not the past.

Past Progressive Tense
Time Dimension: Past; Time Circumstance: In-Progress

Form	Auxiliary Verb (to be) in the Simple Past Tense
	I was, you were, he/she/it was, we/you/they were
	+
	Present Participle (--ing) Form of the verb

Function	
	➢ Action, occurrence, or state of being that was **in-progress in the past**
	The students **were working** on a grammar exercise.
	➢ Action, occurrence, or state of being that was **in-progress in the past** when another action happened
	The students **were working** on a grammar exercise when the fire alarm went off.
	➢ Action, occurrence, or state of being that was **in-progress simultaneously** with another action in the past
	The dedicated students **were** still **working** on the grammar exercise while the fire alarm **was blaring**.
	In all of these cases, the emphasis is on the in-progress effect of the action in the past.

Past Perfect Tense
Time Dimension: Past; Time Circumstance: Perfection

Form	Auxiliary Verb (to have) in the Simple Past Tense
	I/you/he/she/it had, we/you/they had
	+
	Past Participle (--ed) Form of the verb (*for regular verbs)

Function	
	➢ Action, occurrence, or state of being that **was perfected in the past before another action also in the past** (by the point of this other past action)
	Students **had worked** on a grammar exercise in class when the fire alarm went off.
	Here, the students completed the grammar exercise first, and then the alarm went off. The emphasis is on the perfection of the first action in the past by the time another action in the past happened.
	(In the Past Progressive Tense "were working", the students had not completed the exercise when the alarm went off. They were still doing it. Their action was not perfected, but it was still in-progrees.)

Past Perfect Progressive Tense
Time Dimension: Past; Time Circumstance: Continuation/Duration

Form	Auxiliary Verb (to be) in the Past Perfect Tense *I/you/he/she/it had been, we/you/they had been* + Present Participle (--ing) Form of the verb
Function	➢ Action, occurrence, or state of being that started at a certain point in the past but **was not perfected** by the time another action happened; it was still **in-progress in the past**. Students **had been working** on a grammar exercise for twenty minutes when the fire alarm went off. *Here, the students started working on a grammar exercise twenty minutes before the alarm went off; when this happened, they had not completed their work on the exercise; they were still working on it. The **emphasis is** on the **continuation/duration** of the action **between two distinct points in the past**. Actually, it was still in-progress by a certain point the past.* *(In the Past Progressive Tense "were working", the emphasis is not on the continuation/duration of the action in the past; rather, it is on the in-progress effect of the action between two points in the past.)*

Highlight Points:

Past Perfect Tense vs. Present Perfect Tense

What is the real difference? These two tenses might be confusing sometimes, but following the rules about the time dimension and time circumstances of the action, occurrence, or state of being of the verb can solve possible problems. Both tenses put emphasis on the perfection of an action by a certain point in time: in the Present Perfect Tense the point of perfection is in the present while in the Past Perfect Tense the point of perfection is in the past.

➢ Present Perfect Tense:

*Students **have worked** on a grammar exercise today.*
*Here, the action started in the past and has been perfected by a certain point in the present. The emphasis, then, is on the **perfection** of the action **by a certain point in the present**. Actually, the verb tense informs us that the students have finished a grammar exercise today.*

➢ Past Perfect Tense:

*Students had **worked** on a grammar exercise by the time the alarm went off. .*
*Here, the action started in the past and was perfected by a certain point in the past (before another event in the past). The emphasis, then, is on the **perfection** of the action **by a certain point in the past not the present**. Actually, the verb tense informs us that the students had finished a grammar exercise in the past before the alarm went off.*

Travelogue

June 24th, 2006
Mrs. Evridiki, Greece

By the time I **met** (Simple Past) her at 11:00 AM, Mrs. Evridiki **had already been working** (Past Perfect Progressive) for six hours. She **had already milked** (Past Perfect) the goats, **gathered** (Past Perfect) eggs from the chicken coop, **swept** (Past Perfect) and

mopped (Past Perfect) the kitchen, and **prepared** (Past Perfect) three delicious food dishes by the time we **arrived** (Simple Past) at her house in the village of Meskla. To do all this, she **set** (Simple Past) her alarm clock the previous night to her normal waking hour of 5:00 AM. However, the most impressive thing about her **was** (Simple Past) that she **did not consider** (Simple Past) all her labors as extraordinary. Rather, she **thought** (Simple Past) them to be mundane and quotidian. Instead, she **inquired** (Simple Past) about my English teaching job in America and **expressed** (Simple Past) her admiration for my intellectual profession. When she **praised** (Simple Past) me, I **was thinking** (Past Progressive) to myself that despite her name, Euridice, meaning fair in judgment, she **was being** (Past Progressive) unjust to herself because she **considered** (Simple Past) her manual work as inferior to my intellectual labor. On the contrary, I **marveled** (Simple Past) at her knowledge of the land and the animals, and I **was** (Simple Past) able to enjoy her excellent cooking even more because I soon **learned** (Simple Past) that she not only **made** (Simple Past) every dish from scratch, but she also **grew** (Simple Past) all the ingredients.

Harvesting Olives

In my father's village, the olive trees **stand** like ancient sentinels, some of them two hundred years old or more, their boughs laden with their burden. The first day I **joined** the harvest was November 8th, 1985. By dawn, we had already finished a breakfast of bits of bread soaked in olive oil and tomatoes, which my farther had sprinkled with fresh wild oregano. When the village bell struck 7:00 AM, we were already standing in the grove with long rake-like tools in hand. The process was not particularly hard, but there were steps to be taken with care. After we had ensured that the tightly woven nylon netting was spread and secure underneath the olive trees, we proceeded with the long rake and slowly passed the tool through the limbs and leaves of the tree. We had to be careful not to apply too much pressure for fear of breaking a branch and injuring the tree. Since I was the shortest one, my father assigned me with the low limbs of the younger trees. While I was imagining that I was brushing the green hair of some giant, ripe olives were dropping like heavy rain onto the nets until collection later in the day. By dusk, our backs had been aching for hours, but we did not stop until the work was complete. Even to this day, I will always remember my day of initiation into "real" manual work.

Practice with the Past

1. Identify all the verbs in the text by underlining them.

2. Make four separate columns: a) list all verbs in the Simple Past—*e.g. joined*; b) list all verbs in the Past Progressive; c) list all verbs in the Past Perfect; d) list all verbs in the Past Perfect Progressive.

3. Next to each verb in the chart you have assembled, convert the past verb form into its present and future equivalents. Make sure to retain the same number and person of the verb— *e.g. (The first day I) joined (Simple Past); join (Simple Present); will join (Simple Future).*

4. Choose one of your personal favorite pictures and write a story about it as if it happened in the past. Be sure to include details of who, what, when, where, how, and why. Try to use as many past verb tenses as you can correctly.

Vineyard

Before the olives, we always *gathered* the grapes.
Simple Past Tense/ Repetition

Simple Future Tense
Time Dimension: Future; Time Circumstance: Repetition

Form	Auxiliary Verb (will) *I/you/he/she/it will, we/you/they will* + Simple Form of the verb
Function	➢ Habitual action, occurrence, or state of being in the future She **will** always **treasure** her time in college. ➢ Action, occurrence, or state of being that will happen in the future Students **will work** on a verb tense exercise tomorrow.

Future Progressive Tense
Time Dimension: Future; Time Circumstance: In-Progress

Form	Auxiliary Verb (to be) in the Simple Future Tense *I /you/he/she/it will be, we/you/they will be* + Present Participle (--ing) Form of the verb
Function	➢ Action, occurrence, or state of being that will be **in-progress in the future** The students **will be working** on a grammar exercise at 2:30 p.m. tomorrow. *Here, the emphasis is on the in-progress effect of the action in the future.*

Future Perfect Tense
Time Dimension: Future; Time Circumstance: Perfection

Form	Auxiliary Verb (to have) in the Simple Future Tense *I/you/he/she/it will have, we/you/they will have* + Past Participle (--ed) Form of the verb
Function	➢ Action, occurrence, state of being that **will be perfected by a certain point in the future** By next month students **will have worked** on verb tenses for three consecutive weeks. *Here, the students will have perfected working on verb tenses by a certain point in the future (next month). The emphasis is on the perfection of the action in the future.*

Future Perfect Progressive Tense
Time Dimension: Future; Time Circumstance: Continuation/Duration

Form	Auxiliary Verb (to be) in the Future Perfect Tense *I/you/he/she/it will have been, we/you/they will have been* + Present Participle (--ing) Form of the verb
Function	➢ Action, occurrence, state of being that started at a certain point in the past but will not be **perfected** by the time another action will happen; it will still be **in-progress**. By the end of the quarter, students **will have been working** on verb tenses for three weeks. *Here, the students started working on verb tenses three weeks before the end of the quarter; by the end of the quarter, they will still not have completed their work on verb tenses. They will still be working on verb tenses. The **emphasis** is on the **continuation/duration** of the action **between two distinct points in time**. Actually, it will still be in-progress by a certain point in the future.*

Travelogue

June 25th, 2006

Departure, Greece

By tomorrow evening, I **will have spent** (Future Perfect) two weeks in Greece. So, what **will** I **take** (Simple Future) away from the experience? **Will** others back home **recognize** (Simple Future) changes in me after this trip? I certainly **will be** (Simple Future) able to tell them stories and to show them pictures about not only the land but also the people. Back In the U. S., I **will be thinking** (Future Progressive) of my departure and the view from Souda Bay for some time to come. I **will miss** (Simple Future) the peculiar sights and sounds as well as the strong people of Crete. However, I **will try** (Simple Future) to at least cook some of the Cretan dishes of Mrs. Evridiki to remember the tastes from this land. If anything, I **will have** (Simple Future) memories and stories to tell until my next trip.

Merits of Manual Work

There **will** always **be** something distinctly enjoyable and rejuvenating about working with one's hands. Indeed, by the time the manual worker will be done, he will have experienced a gradual satisfaction, so he will eventually feel a sense of completion of a job that at first seemed insurmountable. But it is not simply that at the end of the day, the worker will look back on the work and be thankful it is over. This misses the point entirely. The real satisfaction will have come from working with his hands. In harvesting olives, for instance, the work itself will be part of the pleasure. When each different task will be nearing its end, the harvester will be feeling a distinct satisfaction. The process of harvesting is not something that he will want to avoid as an onerous task, focused entirely on the paycheck at the end. While there will be a finite goal, harvesting olives and producing olive oil, the man, who will have been laboring with his hands all day, will by the end of the day have enjoyed the process of that labor as well as the active working towards producing something. There will always be an element of craftsmanship in shaping the growth of these trees and in gathering their produce to create flavorful oils.

Practice with the Future

1. Identify all the verbs in the text by underlining them.

2. Make four separate columns on: a) list all verbs in the Simple Future—*e.g. will be*; b) list all verbs in the Future Progressive; c) list all verbs in the Future Perfect; d) list all verbs in the Future Perfect Progressive.

3. Next to each verb in the chart you have assembled, convert the future verb form into its present and past equivalents. Make sure to retain the same number and person of the verb—*e.g. (There...something) will be (Simple Future); is (Simple Present); was (Simple Past)*.

4. Choose one of your personal favorite pictures and write a story about it as if it will happen in the future. Be sure to include details of who, what, when, where, how, and why. Try to use as many future verb tenses as you can correctly.

Wine Barrels

After harvesting the grapes, we *will put* the grape juice into barrels.
Simple Future Tense

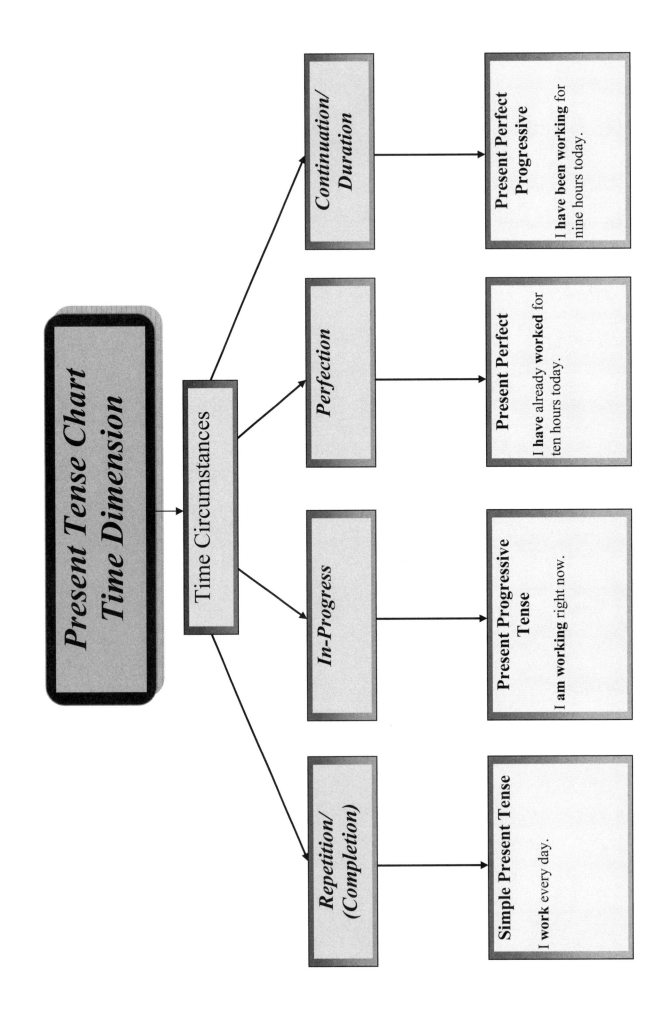

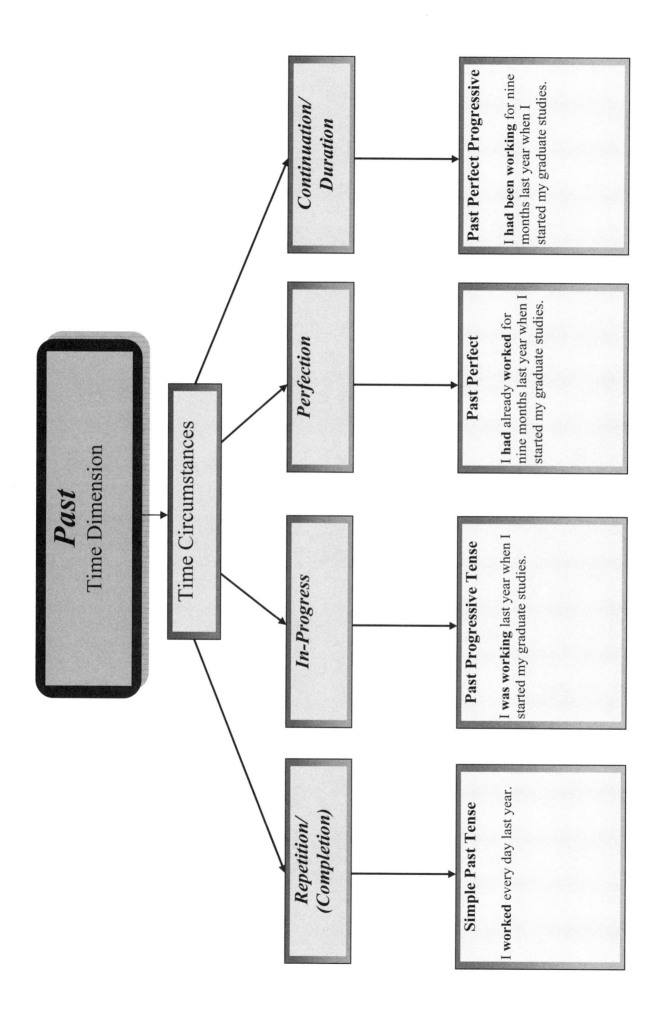

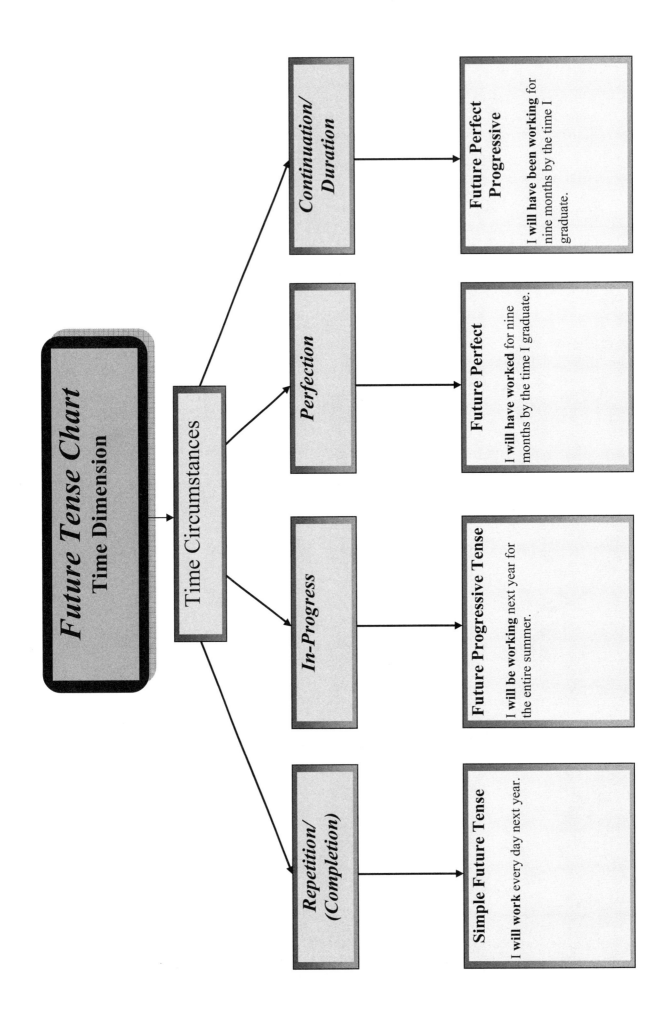

Future Tense Chart
Time Dimension

Time Circumstances

Repetition/ (Completion)

In-Progress

Perfection

Continuation/ Duration

Simple Future Tense

I will work every day next year.

Future Progressive Tense

I will be working next year for the entire summer.

Future Perfect

I will have worked for nine months by the time I graduate.

Future Perfect Progressive

I will have been working for nine months by the time I graduate.

Chapter 2: Irregular Verb Chart

Base	Past Tense	Past Participle
arise	arose	arisen
awake	awoke	awoken
be	was, were	been
bear	bore	born (or borne)
beat	beat	beaten
become	became	become
begin	began	begun
bend	bent	bent
bet	bet	bet
bid (offer)	bid	bid
bid (command)	bade	bidden
bind	bound	bound
bite	bit	bitten
blow	blew	blown
break	broke	broken
bring	brought	brought
build	built	built
burst	burst	burst
buy	bought	bought
cast	cast	cast
catch	caught	caught
choose	chose	chosen
cling	clung	clung
come	came	come
cost	cost	cost
creep	crept	crept
cut	cut	cut
deal	dealt	dealt
dig	dug	dug
dive	dived or dove	dived
do	did	done
draw	drew	drawn
drink	drank	drunk
drive	drove	driven
eat	ate	eaten
fall	fell	fallen
feed	fed	fed
feel	felt	felt
fight	fought	fought
find	found	found
flee	fled	fled
fling	flung	flung
fly	flew	flown
forbid	forbade	forbidden
forget	forgot	forgotten
forgive	forgave	forgiven
forsake	forsook	forsaken
freeze	froze	frozen
get	got	gotten
give	gave	given
go	went	gone
grow	grew	grown
hang	hung	hung
have	had	had
hear	heard	heard
hide	hid	hidden
hit	hit	hit
hurt	hurt	hurt
keep	kept	kept
know	knew	known
lay	laid	laid
lead	led	led
leave	left	left
lend	lent	lent
let	let	let
lie	lay	lain
light	lighted or lit	lighted or lit
lose	lost	lost
make	made	made
mean	meant	meant
pay	paid	paid
prove	proved	proven
quit	quit	quit
read	read	read
rid	rid	rid
ride	rode	ridden
ring	rang	rung
rise	rose	risen
run	ran	run
say	said	said
see	saw	seen
seek	sought	sought
send	sent	sent
set	set	set
shake	shook	shaken
shine	shone	shone
shoot	shot	shot
show	showed	shown
shrink	shrank	shrunk
sing	sang	sung
sink	sank	sunk
sit	sat	sat
slay	slew	slain
sleep	slept	slept
sling	slung	slung
speak	spoke	spoken
spend	spent	spent
spin	spun	spun
spring	sprang	sprung
stand	stood	stood
steal	stole	stolen
sting	stung	stung
stink	stank	stunk
stride	strode	stridden
strike	struck	struck
strive	strove	striven
swear	swore	sworn
sweep	swept	swept
swim	swam	swum
swing	swung	swung
take	took	taken
teach	taught	taught
tear	tore	torn
tell	told	told
think	thought	thought
throw	threw	thrown
understand	understood	understood
wake	woke	woken
wear	wore	worn
write	wrote	written

MOST COMMON AUXILIARY VERBS:
TO BE, TO DO, TO HAVE

TO BE

	PRESENT	PAST	FUTURE
Simple	I **am**	I **was**	I **will be**
	you **are**	you **were**	you will be
	he/she/it **is**	he/she/it **was**	he/she/it will be
	we/you/they are	we/you/they were	we/you/they will be
Progressive	I **am being**	I **was being**	very rare
	you **are being**	you **were being**	
	he/she/it **is being**	he/she/it **was being**	
	we/you/they are being	we/you/they were being	
Perfect	I **have been**	I **had been**	I **will have been**
	you have been	you had been	you will have been
	he/she/it **has been**	he/she/it had been	he/she/it will have been
	we/you/they have been	we/you/they had been	we/you/they will have been
Perfect Progressive	I **have been being**	I **had been being**	I **will have been being**
	very rare	very rare	very rare

TO DO

	PRESENT	PAST	FUTURE
Simple	I **do**	I **did**	I **will do**
	you do	you did	you will do
	he/she/it **does**	he/she/it did	he/she/it will do
	we/you/they do	we/you/they did	we/you/they will do
Progressive	I **am doing**	I **was doing**	I **will be doing**
	you are doing	you were doing	you will be doing
	he/she/it is doing	he/she/it **was doing**	he/she/it will be doing
	we/you/they are doing	we/you/they were doing	we/you/they will be doing
Perfect	I **have done**	I **had done**	I **will have done**
	you have done	you had done	you will have done
	he/she/it **has done**	he/she/it had done	he/she/it will have done
	we/you/they have done	we/you/they had done	we/you/they will have done
Perfect Progressive	I **have been doing**	I **had been doing**	I **will have been doing**
	you have been doing	you had been doing	you will have been doing
	he/she/it **has been doing**	he/she/it had been doing	he/she/it will have been doing
	we/you/they have been doing	we/you/they had been doing	we/you/they will have been doing

TO HAVE

	PRESENT	PAST	FUTURE
Simple	I **have**	I **had**	I **will have**
	you have	you had	you will have
	he/she/it **has**	he/she/it had	he/she/it will have
	we/you/they have	we/you/they had	we/you/they will have
Progressive	I **am having**	I **was having**	I **will be having**
	you **are having**	you **were having**	you will be having
	he/she/it **is having**	he/she/it **was having**	he/she/it will be having
	we/you/they are having	we/you/they were having	we/you/they will be having
Perfect	I **have done**	I **had done**	I **will have done**
	you have done	you had done	you will have done
	he/she/it **has done**	he/she/it had done	he/she/it will have done
	we/you/they have done	we/you/they had done	we/you/they will have done
Perfect Progressive	I **have been having**	I **had been having**	I **will have been doing**
	you have been having	you had been having	**very rare**
	he/she/it **has been having**	he/she/it had been having	
	we/you/they have been having	we/you/they had been having	

Chapter 3
Sentence Structures
Units of Meaning

Parts of speech are the building blocks of language, and they are used to construct units of meaning that ultimately serve communication. In English, there are certain distinct categories of such units of meaning: **clauses, phrases, and sentences**. To construct meaning that is coherent and comprehensible to others, one needs to be familiar with both the form and the function of these units of meaning as well as to follow certain rules about their usage.

Chapter Three—Pyramid: Units of Meaning

Phrase

A group of words that "hang together."

Incomplete Thought=Must be Part of a Clause

EX. *The powerful laptop (noun)* _____.

Clause

Subject +Predicate
Dependent or Independent

Dependent Clause:

Word of Dependence +
Subject + Predicate
=
Incomplete Thought

EX. Because the powerful laptop broke down, _____.
(what happened?)

Independent Clause:

Subject +Predicate
=
Complete Thought
(= Simple Sentence)

EX. The powerful laptop (noun) broke down (predicate).

Sentence

Complete Thought
Minimum Requirement:
1 Independent Clause
May contain one or more clauses

Sentences contain a minimum of 1 Independent Clause.

I broke the laptop **(IC)**.	1 **IC** (Simple)
I broke the laptop **(IC)**, and you fixed it **(IC)**.	2 **IC** (Compound)
Because I broke the laptop (DC), you had to fix it **(IC)**.	1 **DC** + 1 **IC** (Complex)
Because I broke the laptop (DC), you had to fix it **(IC)**, but it cost a lot of money **(IC)**.	1 **DC** + 2 **IC** (Compound / Complex)

PHRASES

PHRASE DEFINITIONS

Formal Definition

Form: Similar to a clause, a phrase is also **a group of related words**; however, it lacks a subject, or a predicate, or both. All phrases, except for absolute ones, are groups of related words that are **based on one main word** (part of speech), whether that be a noun, a verb, a participle, an infinitive, or a preposition. Depending on its basis, a phrase can be a noun, verb, participial, infinitive, or prepositional phrase. One additional type is absolute phrases which modify entire clauses.

Function: A phrase, as a group of related words, functions as one unit of meaning. Furthermore, this unit functions in the exact same way as the particular part of speech it is based on (noun, verb, participle, infinitive, or a preposition). However, this unit is incomplete because it lacks the characteristics of a clause (a subject and a predicate). Therefore, to convey a complete meaning, a phrase needs to be part of a clause.

Etymology: The word *phrase* derives from the Greek word *phrazein*, which means *to express*. This is exactly what phrases do: they express meaning which is, however, incomplete.

Informal Definition

One can easily understand the importance of clauses and other units of meaning just by taking a look at nature. Nature constitutes a system of various units of life (meaning). One of those main units of life (meaning) is trees. As a unit of life (meaning), a tree consists of certain important parts, integral to its existence: roots, a trunk, branches, leaves, even blossoms. Of those parts, what seems to be mostly important and almost always present is the roots, the trunk, and the branches. Some of these elements are more important than others. Since phrases are not an absolutely necessary part of a sentence, they would be a tree's leaves and blossoms, for a tree can survive without them at least for some time.

PHRASE TYPES

Phrases are classified into different types according to their different properties and functions. These properties determine how phrases function within clauses and sentences. Knowing the parts of speech, both in terms of their form and their function, is pivotal to understanding phrases. Depending on which part of speech a phrase is based on, it can belong to one of the following types: **Noun Phrase**, **Verb Phrase**, **Participial Phrase, Infinitive Phrase, and Prepositional Phrase**. The only phrase type that is not based on one part of speech is the **Absolute Phrase**.

Noun Phrases

Form: A noun phrase is a group of related words that is based on a noun.

Function: A noun phrase functions in the same way as a noun. It can be a subject, an object, a subject complement (for more see Parts of Speech: Nouns).

Functions as a subject:

Many American **scientists** are very famous.

"Many American scientists" is one group of related words that is based on the noun "scientists". This noun phrase functions as the complete subject in the clause.

Functions as an object:

The U.S. government has honored many American **scientists**.

"...many American scientists" is one group of related words that is based on the noun "scientists". This noun phrase functions as the object of the transitive verb "has honored".

Functions as a subject complement:

Many American scientists are esteemed university **graduates**.

"...esteemed university graduates" is one group of related words that is based on the noun "graduates". This noun phrase functions as the subject complement of the complete subject "many American scientists".

Verb Phrases

Form: A verb phrase is a group of related words that is based on a verb (with its auxiliary-helping verbs).

Function: A verb phrase functions in the same way as a verb (for more see Parts of Speech: Verbs).

The U.S. government **has** often and diligently **honored** many American scientists.

"...has often and diligently honored" is one group of related words that is based on the verb "has honored". This verb phrase functions as the predicate of the clause.

Participial Phrases

Form: A participial phrase is a group of related words that is based on a participle (present or past).

Function: A participial phrase functions in the same way as a participle (for more see Parts of Speech: Verb Forms).

Present Participle (-ing Form of Verb):

- Functions as a noun (gerund)

Honoring American scientists is a responsibility of the U.S. government.

"Honoring American scientists" is one group of related words that is based on the present participle (gerund) "honoring". This participial phrase functions as a noun and more specifically in this case as the complete subject of the clause.

- Functions as an adjective

Honoring American scientists, the U.S. government bestowed various grants.

"Honoring American scientists" is one group of related words that is based on the present participle "honoring". This participial phrase functions as a modifier (adjective), and it describes the noun "government".

Past Participle (-ed Form of Verb):

- Functions as an adjective

Honored by the U.S. government, the American scientists continued thriving in their field.

"Honored by the U.S. government" is one group of related words that is based on the past participle "honored". This participial phrase functions as a modifier (adjective), and it describes the noun "scientists".

Infinitive Phrases

Form: An infinitive phrase is a group of related words that is based on an infinitive.

Function: An infinitive phrase functions in the same way as an infinitive (for more see Parts of Speech: Verb Forms).

Functions as a noun:

To honor American scientists is a responsibility of the U.S. government.

"To honor American scientists" is one group of related words that is based on the infinitive "to honor". This infinitive phrase functions as a noun and more specifically in this case as the complete subject of the clause.

Functions as an adjective:

The U.S. government took the initiative **to honor** certain American scientists.

"...to honor certain American scientists" is one group of related words that is based on the infinitive "to honor". This infinitive phrase functions as a modifier (adjective), and it describes the noun "initiative".

Functions as an adverb:

The U.S. government was right **to honor** certain American scientists.

"...to honor certain American scientists" is one group of related words that is based on the infinitive "to honor". This infinitive phrase functions as a modifier (adverb of manner), and it modifies the adjective "right".

Prepositional Phrases

Form: A prepositional phrase is a group of related words that is based on a preposition.

Function: A prepositional phrase functions in the same way as a preposition (for more see Parts of Speech: Prepositions).

Functions as an adjective:

Honoring American scientists is a responsibility **of** the U.S. government.

"...of the U.S. government" is one group of related words that is based on the preposition "of". This prepositional phrase functions as a modifier (adjective) that describes the noun "responsibility".

Functions as an adverb:

The U.S. government honored certain American scientists **in** a glamorous ceremony.

"...in a glamorous ceremony" is one group of related words that is based on the preposition "in". This prepositional phrase functions as a modifier (adverb of manner), and it modifies the verb "honored".

As an adverb:

The U.S. government was right **to honor** certain American scientists.

"...to honor certain American scientists" is one group of related words that is based on the infinitive "to honor". This infinitive phrase functions as a modifier (adverb of manner), and it modifies the adjective "right".

Absolute Phrases

Form: An absolute phrase is a group of related words that does not have one particular word as its basis. It usually consists of a noun or a pronoun, and a present or a past participle, and their modifiers.

Function: An absolute phrase functions as a modifier to an entire clause and not just one element in a clause.

Guests gathering from all fields of science, the ceremony turned out to be glamorous.

"Guests gathering from all fields of science" is one group of related words. This absolute phrase functions as a modifier (adverb), and it modifies the whole clause "the ceremony...glamorous". .

Their research completed, the American scientists received their awards.

"Their research completed" is one group of related words. This absolute phrase functions as a modifier (adverb), and it modifies the whole clause "the American scientists...awards"..

Travelogue

July 12th, 2005
Death Valley

To visit (infinitive) Death Valley in the summer is beyond me, but since I was on my way to the Grand Canyon, I thought I would take a detour to one of the most famous national parks in the United States. Having an apt name and the highest recorded temperature in the U.S. (134 degrees) (Participial), Death Valley seems inhospitable to nearly every living creature. Found some four hours drive north east of Los Angeles, (Participial) Death Valley is the hottest, driest, and lowest place in the Western Hemisphere. The valley itself gets its name from the fateful Donner party of 1849-1850 who were a group of settlers. Traversing the Sierra Nevada mountain range, (Participial) they ran out of supplies by the time they reached Death Valley. Driving through the mile upon mile of empty terrain, (Participial) I imagined how difficult it would be to survive (infinitive) in such a climate. Having this in mind, (Participial) I was amazed that there had been people who lived in Death Valley permanently, despite the ferocious heat in the summer and cold in the winter. Yet people came in the early 1900s for the borax found in the mountain ranges nearby, their water hauled from distant towns (Absolute). To do so (infinitive) created one more story of people's desire to tame nature (infinitive). As for me, I only dared tame nature through the confines of my air-conditioned car.

Only participial, infinitive, and absolute phrases have been marked.

The Grand Canyon

The Grand Canyon is a completely awe- inspiring place, mere words being insufficient to capture. It is something that must be experienced first hand, for photographs or films, though artfully and skillfully executed, can only approximate the grandeur of this monumental canyon. Quantifying its grandeur with numbers can of course help us put things into perspective...but only a little. Measured at over 277 miles long, a mile deep, and in places 18 miles wide, this gorge was carved over millions of years by the Colorado River, and it is now part of a beltway of seven national parks spreading out into parts of Utah, Colorado, Idaho, and Arizona. Dwarfing other natural formations in its colossal dimensions, the Grand Canyon is aptly named. However, the Grand Canyon is far more than the sum of its size. To visit the Canyon is about experiencing the sublime, about connecting with our own spiritual selves. However, above all it is about relearning that humans are but a part of nature.

Practice with Phrases

1. Make six separate columns: a) list all noun phrases; b) list all verb phrases; c) list all participial phrases; d) list all infinitive phrases; e) list all prepositional phrases; f) list all absolute phrases.

2. In each one of the above phrases, underline the main word (part of speech) that is the basis of the phrase.

3. On a separate sheet of paper, try to convert phrases into clauses whenever possible.

The magnificent Grand Canyon...

Noun Phrase

Admiring the view...

Participial (Gerund) Phrase

Chapter Three—Mini Review: Phrases

Phrases

A Group of Related Words

Smaller than Clauses and Sentences

- Phrases are the **mini units of meaning** that help "make up" clauses.
- Phrases form a group of words that hang together **based on one central word** with the exception of absolute phrases.
- Phrases function in the **exact same way** as the part of speech they are based on.
- Phrases **DO NOT** convey a complete thought, so they cannot stand by themselves.

Noun Phrase

Subject   *Many enrolled <u>students</u>* study their notes.

Object   The university bills *many enrolled <u>students</u>*.

Complement   Many students are *great and insightful <u>writers</u>*.

Verb Phrase

Diligent students *<u>must always study</u> long hours.*

The university *adamantly <u>bills</u>* many enrolled students.

Participial Phrase

- *<u>Studying diligently</u>* helps students get better grades. (as a noun: Gerund)

-ing form

- *<u>Studying diligently</u>*, the "A" students passed the exam. (as an adjective)

- *<u>Billed for the tuition</u>*, the students had no money left. (as an adjective)

-ed form

Infinitive Phrase

Noun   *<u>To study</u> notes diligently* is not easy.

Adjective   Students have many notes *<u>to study</u> diligently*.

Adverb   Many students try hard *<u>to study</u> diligently*.

Prepositional Phrase

Adjective   The students *<u>from the class</u>* studied together.

Adverb   The students sat *<u>near the bell tower</u>*.

Absolute Phrase

***modifies an entire clause and is separated from the clause with a comma:

The notes studied and the tests taken, the students went on spring break.

CLAUSES

CLAUSE DEFINITIONS

Formal Definition

Form: A clause is a group of related words that must include a subject and a predicate. Clauses can be independent, or they can be dependent in case they are accompanied by words that create dependence (subordinating conjunctions, relative pronouns).

Function: As a group of related words, a clause conveys meaning about a subject performing an action (predicate), about something (subject) happening (predicate), or about a subject in a certain state of being (predicate).

Etymology: The word *clause* derives from the Latin word *claudere*, meaning *to close*. This is exactly what clauses do: they close off or separate these units of meaning from other ones.

Informal Definition

One can easily understand the importance of clauses and other units of meaning just by taking a look at nature. Nature constitutes a system of various units of life (meaning). One of those main units of life (meaning) is trees. As a unit of life (meaning), a tree consists of certain important parts, integral to its existence: roots, a trunk, branches, leaves, even blossoms. Of those parts, what seems to be mostly important and almost always present is the roots, the trunk, and the branches. Some of these elements are more important than others. Since independent clauses are what holds everything together, they would be the tree's roots and trunk. Dependent clauses, though important, need to depend on the roots and the trunk for their existence; therefore, dependent clauses would be the tree's branches.

CLAUSE CHARACTERISTICS

All clauses must have a subject and a predicate; otherwise, they are incomplete units of meaning (see phrases). The **subject** of a clause conveys information about who or what performs an action, happens, or exists in a state of being. A subject can be simple, compound, and complete.

All clauses must have a **predicate**; otherwise, they are incomplete units of meaning (see phrases). The main and necessary component of any predicate is a verb because the predicate conveys information about the action, the occurrence, or the state of being of a certain subject. However, although the predicate of a clause is based on a verb, it may include more elements that accompany or modify the verb. Like subjects, predicates can be simple, compound, and complete.

Simple Subject

Definition	Example
A simple subject consists of one noun or pronoun or words that function as nouns or pronouns such as gerunds and infinitives. All of these words need to be in the subjective case (see Parts of Speech: Nouns).	**Scientists** observe nature. (*Subject: Noun*) **They** record their observations. (*Subject: Pronoun*) **Observing** nature requires diligence. (*Subject: Gerund that functions as a noun*) **To observe** nature requires diligence. (*Subject: Infinitive that functions as a noun*)

Compound Subject

Definition	Example
A compound subject consists of two or more nouns or pronouns or words that function as nouns or pronouns such as gerunds and infinitives which are connected with the coordinating conjunction "and".	**Scientists** and **researchers** observe nature. (*Subject: Nouns*) **She and I** record our observations. (*Subject: Pronouns*) **Observing** and **recording** nature require diligence. (*Subject: Gerunds that function as nouns*) **To observe** and **to record** nature require diligence. (*Subject: Infinitives that function as nouns*)

Complete Subject

Definition	Example

Scientists from the University of California observe natur*e*.

A complete subject is a simple or a compound subject that is accompanied by various modifiers such as adjectives or prepositional phrases. These modifiers do not change the subject's character as simple or compound.

*The noun "Scientists" is the simple subject of the clause. Furthermore, this simple subject is accompanied by the prepositional phrase "from...California" that functions as a modifier (adjective). Together with its modifier, the simple subject forms the **complete simple subject** of the clause.*

German **scientists** and French **environmentalists** observe nature.

Simple does not necessarily mean one word; it means one noun or pronoun acting as a subject. The subject, either simple or compound, together with its modifiers is called the "**Complete Subject**".

*The nouns "scientists" and "environmentalists" combined by the conjunction "and" form the compound subject of the clause. Furthermore, each noun is accompanied by the modifiers (adjectives) "German" and "French". Together with their modifiers, the nouns of the compound subject form the **complete compound subject** of the clause.*

Highlight Points:

A. Clauses vs. Sentences

Clauses are the units of meaning that help us construct sentences. Sentences can consist of one or more clauses. Therefore, a complete sentence needs at least one set of a subject and a predicate (one clause which has to be independent; for more see Sentence Structures: Sentences). However, a sentence may have more than one set of subjects and predicates (clauses).

B. Significance of the Complete Subject

Identifying the complete subject helps us determine the boundaries of each clause, so we avoid errors such as fragments, comma splices, run-on sentences as well as errors in subject/verb agreement. This is very important in case a sentence has more than one clause.

C. Finding the Subject of a Clause

Although the subject usually comes first in a clause (unless the clause is a question or an idiomatic structure), one needs to first find the verb of the predicate in the clause in order to find the subject. Then, one needs to ask the question "Who or What is performing the action of the verb?", "What is the occurrence of the verb?", or "Who or What is in a specific state of being of the verb?" The answer to these questions will reveal the subject of the clause.

D. Conjunctions and Compound Subjects

Identifying a subject as compound is important because a compound subject requires a verb in the plural (for more see Subject/Verb Agreement).

Simple Predicate

Definition	Example
A simple predicate is based on a verb which shows action, occurrence, or state of being. Simple predicates consist of one verb, which may also include an auxiliary (helping) verb.	Scientists **observe** nature. *(Verb of Simple Predicate: observe)*
	They **are recording** their observations. *(Verb of Simple Predicate: are recording)*
	Observing nature **may require** diligence. *(Verb of Simple Predicate: may require)*

Compound Predicate

Definition	Example
A compound predicate is based on verbs which shows action, occurrence, or state of being. A compound predicate consists of two or more verbs, which may include auxiliary (helping) verbs. Compound predicates are joined by conjunctions (**Coordinating**: For, And, Nor, But, Or, Yet, So; **Correlative**: neither/nor, either/or, not only/but also)	Scientists **observe** and **respect** nature. *(Verbs of Compound Predicate: observe, respect)*
	They **are recording** and **processing** their observations. *(Verbs of Compound Predicate: are recording, (are) processing)*
	Observing nature **may require** diligence and **may last** long. *(Verbs of Compound Predicate: may require, may last)*

Complete Predicate

A complete predicate is either a simple or a compound predicate that is accompanied by various modifiers such as adverbs and prepositional phrases, as well as objects (direct and indirect) and subject complements. These additional elements do not change the predicate's character as simple or compound. Simple does not necessarily mean one word; it means one verb as the basis of the predicate. The predicate, either simple or compound, together with its modifiers is called the "**Complete Predicate**".

Types	Example
Verb + Modifiers	**Simple Complete Predicate** Natural phenomena **occur** constantly. *(Intransitive) Verb(occur) + Modifier-Adverb of frequency (constantly)* **Compound Complete Predicate** Natural phenomena **occur** constantly and **change** with time. *1st (Intransitive) Verb(occur)+ Modifier-Adverb of frequency (constantly)* *+ (and)* *2nd (Intransitive) Verb (change)+Prepositional Phrase-Adverb of manner(with time)*
(Transitive) Verb + Object(s)	**Simple Complete Predicate** Scientists **observe** nature. *Transitive Verb (observe) + Direct Object (nature)* Scientists **send** committees their findings. *Transitive Verb (send) + Indirect Object (committees) + Direct Object (their findings)* **Compound Complete Predicate** Scientists **observe** nature and **record** their findings. *1st Transitive Verb (observe) + 1st Direct Object (nature)* *+ (and)* *2nd Transitive Verb (record) + 2nd Direct Object (their findings).* Scientists **send** committees their findings and **offer** environmentalists their results. *1st Transitive Verb (observe)+ 1st Indirect Object (committees) + 1st Direct Object (nature)* *+ (and)* *2nd Transitive Verb (record) + 2nd Indirect Object (environmentalists) + 2nd Direct Object (their results).*

Simple Complete Predicate

Many environmentalists **are** <u>scientists</u>.

Linking verb (are) + (Noun) Subject Complement (scientists)

Scientists **are** <u>very meticulous</u>.

Linking verb (are) + (Adjective) Subject Complement (very <u>meticulous</u>)

Compound Complete Predicate

Many people **are** <u>scientists at first</u> and then **become** <u>environmentalists</u>.

1st Linking verb (are) + 1st (Noun) Subject Complement (scientists)

+ (and)

2nd Linking Verb (become) + 2nd (Noun) Subject Complement (environmentalists)

Scientists **are** <u>very studious</u> and often **seem** <u>distraught</u>.

1st Linking verb (are) + 1st (Adjective) Subject Complement (very studious)

+ (and)

2nd Linking Verb (seem) + 2nd (Adjective) Subject Complement (distraught)

(Linking) Verb + Subject Complement

Highlight Points:

A. Predicates vs. Verbs

Verbs and predicates are often confused, but the distinction is quite easy. Verbs are the basis of predicates. No predicate can exist without a verb. However, a predicate can consist of only (one or more) verbs, or it can also include other elements such as verb modifiers (adverbs, prepositional phrases, etc), objects, and/or subject complements.

B. Significance of the Complete Predicate

Identifying the complete predicate helps one determine the boundaries of each clause, so one can avoid errors such as fragments, comma splices, run-on sentences. This is very important in case a sentence has more than one clause.

C. Finding the Predicate of a Clause

Although in a clause the subject usually comes first and the verb second (unless it's a question or an idiomatic structure), one needs to first find the verb of the predicate in the clause. To do so, one needs to look both at the form and the function of certain words in the clause. Verbs will be the words that convey information about an action, occurrence, or state of being; however, these words also need to be in those verb forms that function as verbs, not nouns or adjectives (for more see Parts of Speech: Verb Forms).

D. Transitive vs. Intransitive Verbs

Transitive verbs require an object to complete their meaning. The energy of these verbs is **transferred** to their object.

> *Scientists **observe nature**.*

> *The energy of the verb "observe" transfers to the object "nature".*

Intransitive verbs do not require an object to complete their meaning. The energy of these verbs remains within the verb and its subject; it is **not transferred** to an object *(for more information see Parts of Speech: Verbs)*.

> *Nature **changes** constantly.*

> *The energy of the verb "changes" is not transferred; it remains within the verb and its subject.*

E. Direct vs. Indirect Objects

Transitive verbs can take both a direct and an indirect object. As the terms indicate, a direct object is the one that receives the energy of the verb directly (the first one to receive it) while the indirect object is the one that receives the energy of the verb indirectly (the second one to receive it). However, usually the indirect object is placed first and is followed by the direct object. Also, the indirect object is found if one asks the questions "to whom?" or "for whom"?

> *Scientists send **committees** their **findings**.*

> *The energy of the verb "send" transfers first to the direct object "findings" and then to the indirect object "committees". To whom do scientists send their findings? To the "committees"(indirect object).*

F. Linking Verbs and Subject Complements

Linking verbs connect the subject of a clause to a complement. They operate as equal signs (=) in an equation between the subject and its complement.

A complement, whether it be a noun, an adjective, a pronoun, or a clause, completes the subject in some way (*for more information, see Parts of Speech: Verbs*).

> *Scientists **are** very **meticulous**.*

> *The linking verb "are" connects the subject "Scientists" to its complement "meticulous".*

Travelogue

July 10th, 2005

Escaping Southern California

After I (subject) had completed (verb) a long year of hard work, I (subject) thought (verb) that I (subject) deserved (verb) some rest, relaxation, and renewal. I (subject) was feeling (verb) very tired of the crowds and the hectic traffic of Southern California, so I (subject) decided (verb) to do what millions (subject) of Americans do (verb) every year: escape suburbia by taking a road trip. Of course, the magic (subject) of a road trip is (verb) having an ultimate destination as well as having the time to wander off the beaten track. I (subject) opened (verb) my atlas, closed (verb) my

eyes, and hoped (verb) that my finger (subject) would find (verb) some interesting place to visit. Well, my first venture (subject) with this method would have placed (verb) me in the Gobi desert in China. I (subject) had (verb) neither the inclination nor the money to go into the Gobi desert, so I (subject) tried (verb) again; the second time I (subject) was (verb) luckier. My destination (subject) was (verb) the Grand Canyon. After checking the car, packing the bags, and finding a cat sitter, I (subject) set off (verb) to escape the asphalt and concrete jungle of suburbia. This (subject) was (verb) not easy, for the freeways (subject) were (verb) like clogged arteries. I (subject) just kept (verb) telling myself to be patient, and soon I (subject) would be (verb) on the open road.

Americans and Nature

The American *psyche* <u>reveals</u> a schizophrenic relationship with nature. On the one hand, Americans revere national parks such as The Grand Canyon; on the other hand, Americans insist on living patterns which do not preserve the natural environment. Overall, Americans have a desire to conquer nature. However, this desire for conquest often is synonymous with vast needs and wasteful consumption. All of these threaten and exhaust natural resources. For instance, one can see uncontrolled housing projects in the Southern California area; these projects cover vast stretches of land with suburbs, and they gradually swallow whole mountain ranges and gulp down water reservoirs. In the name of growth and profit, every year developers and constructors completely alter land. At the same time, environmentalists accept poor agreements which set aside only small reserve areas. In these reserve areas no one can build, and people can visit on the weekends. These areas are a sad testament to what the landscape looked like before human intervention.

Practice with Subjects and Predicates

1. Identify all the verbs in the text by underlining them, including the auxiliary verbs—*e.g. reveals.*

2. Identify all the complete predicates and make three separate columns: a) list all predicates (verb(s) + modifiers); b) list all predicates (verb(s) + object(s)). c) list all predicates (verb(s) + subject complements).

3. Identify the subject of each verb in the text by circling them.--*e.g. psyche (The American psyche: complete subject).*

4. Make four separate columns: a) list all simple (complete) subjects, b) list all compound (complete) subjects, c) list all simple (complete) predicates, and d) list all compound (complete) predicates.

Developers (subject)

change the land (predicate).

Vast areas of land (subject)

are agricultural (predicate).

CLAUSE TYPES

Clauses are classified into different types according to their properties. These properties determine how clauses function within sentences. There are two main types of clauses: **Independent** and **Dependent**. The distinction between the two main types relies on their form (the presence or not of words that create dependence) as well as their function (the inclusion or not of complete meaning).

Dependent clauses are further divided into four categories depending either on their function or form: **Adverb**, **Adjective**, **Noun**, and **Elliptical**.

Independent Clause

Form: An independent clause has a subject and a predicate and is characterized by the absence of any words that create dependence (subordinating conjunctions and relative pronouns).

Function: An independent clause forms a complete unit of meaning and can stand on its own.

Scientists observe nature.

Subject (scientists) + Predicate (observe nature) + no words that create dependence = complete meaning

Both scientists and environmentalists observe phenomena and respect nature.

Subject (scientists + environmentalists) + Predicate (observe phenomena + respect nature) + no words that create dependence = complete meaning

Principle: No words that create dependence, complete meaning

Significance: Sentence structure, fragments, comma splices, run-on sentences, mixed constructions

Dependent Clause

Form: A dependent clause has a subject and a predicate and is accompanied by words that create dependence (subordinating conjunctions and relative pronouns).

Function: A dependent clause does not form a complete unit of meaning and cannot stand on its own. Therefore, it always accompanies and relies on an independent clause to complete its meaning.

After scientists observe nature.

Subject (scientists) + Predicate (observe nature) + "after" subordinating conjunction = incomplete meaning

Although both scientists and environmentalists observe phenomena and respect nature.

Subject (scientists + environmentalists) + Predicate (observe phenomena + respect nature) + "although" subordinating conjunction = incomplete meaning

Principle: Words that create dependence, incomplete meaning

Significance: Sentence structure, fragments, comma usage

Adverb (Dependent) Clause

Form: An adverb (dependent) clause usually begins with a subordinating conjunction such as because, since, although, until, if, unless, etc. (for a complete list, see Parts of Speech: Conjunctions).

Function: An adverb (dependent) clause functions as an adverb; therefore, it modifies a verb, an adjective, an adverb, or a clause. This adverb clause explains issues such as: *When? Where? Why? How?* etc.

Modifies a verb:

The scientists presented their data **as** coherently as they could.

*The subordinating conjunction "as" introduces the adverb (dependent) clause "as...could" that modifies the verb "presented". This clause explains **how** the scientists presented their data.*

Modifies an adjective:

The presentation of data was coherent **because** many visuals were included.

*The subordinating conjunction "because" introduces the adverb (dependent) clause "because...included" that modifies the adjective "coherent". This clause explains **why** the presentation was coherent.*

Modifies an adverb:

The scientists presented the data more coherently **than** I could have imagined.

*The subordinating conjunction "than" introduces the adverb (dependent) clause "than...imagined" that modifies the adverb "coherently". This clause explains **how** coherently the data was presented.*

Modifies a clause:

After the scientists presented their data, they published their results.

*The subordinating conjunction "after" introduces the adverb (dependent) clause "after...data" that modifies the clause "they...results". This adverb clause explains **when** the scientists published their results.*

Adjective (Dependent) Clause

Form: An adjective (dependent) clause usually begins with a relative pronoun such as who, whom, whose, which, and that. It can also start with a relative adverb such *when* and *where*. (For a complete list, see: Parts of Speech: Adjectives and Adverbs). These clauses are also called *relative clauses*.

Function: An adjective (dependent) clause functions as a modifier (adjective); therefore, this clause describes a noun or a pronoun or any words that function as nouns or pronouns.

Modifies a noun:

The scientists presented the data **which** <u>they had collected for many years.</u>

The relative pronoun "which" introduces the adjective (dependent) clause "which...years" that modifies the noun "data". This clause describes the noun "data".

Modifies a pronoun:

Those **who** had collected data for many years presented it at the conference.

The relative pronoun "who" introduces the adjective (dependent) clause "who...years" that modifies the pronoun "those". This clause describes the pronoun "those".

Noun (Dependent) Clause

Form: A noun (dependent) clause also usually begins with a relative pronoun such as who, which, that, and their derivatives such as whoever, whichever, etc. It can also start with a relative adverb such how, what, *where, when, and why*. (For a complete list, see: Parts of Speech: Adjectives and Adverbs).

Function: A noun (dependent) clause functions as a noun; therefore, in a sentence a noun clause can be a subject, an object, a complement, etc.

Functions as a subject:

Whoever <u>collected the scientific data</u> presented it at the conference.

The relative pronoun "whoever" introduces the adjective (dependent) clause "whoever...data" that functions as a noun and more specifically as the subject of the verb "presented".

Functions as an object:

Scientists acknowledged whomever they had interviewed during their research.

The relative pronoun "whomever" introduces the noun (dependent) clause "whomever...research" that functions as a noun and more specifically as the object of the verb "acknowledged".

Functions as a complement:

The data presented was **whatever** <u>the scientists had collected for many years.</u>

The relative pronoun "whatever" introduces the noun (dependent) clause "whatever...years" that functions as a noun and more specifically as the complement of the subject "data".

Highlight Points:

Elliptical Dependent clauses

As the term implies (elision of words), elliptical are the dependent clauses in which one or more words have been omitted for conciseness. Even though they are omitted, the meaning and function of these words are usually clear from the context. In most cases of elliptical clauses, the word omitted is the relative pronoun or subordinating conjunction "that".

I understand (that) I need to pay more attention to my instructor.

Here, that could be omitted creating that way an elliptical clause.

Travelogue

July 10th, 2005

Taming Nature: Hoover Dam

[Sitting some thirty miles outside of Las Vegas, rises one of the great modern wonders of the world.]IC (Because I had always read about it but had never seen it,) DC [I detoured from the I-15 freeway to visit the famous Hoover Dam.] IC (Although many photographers have tried to capture the size and scale of this man-made achievement,) DC [none even approached the mark.] IC (Unless one visits Hoover Dam,) DC [one cannot realize its magnitude.] IC [All the numbers about Hoover Dam are immense: 726

feet high, 5 million barrels of concrete, 45 million pounds of steel, and 247 square miles of reservoir in Lake Mead.] IC [These numbers are hard to conceptualize,] IC [but one can at least fathom the quantity of concrete in another way.] IC [Indeed, the amount of concrete (which was used in the dam's construction) DC could build a highway from San Francisco to New York.] IC [This taming of nature did not occur over night] IC (as it required three years of constant labor) DC (in which over 21,000 men participated.) DC [Moreover, these engineers, designers, and workers had to divert the mighty Colorado river] IC (while they were building the dam,) DC (which was no easy task in and of itself.) DC [Last but not least, they had to work in a hostile environment] IC (where the temperature during summer months often reached 130 degrees in the shade;) DC [it was so hot] IC (that workers fried eggs on stones without using a stove.) DC [Hoover Dam is a testament to man's ability to conquer and tame nature to his own uses.] IC

[IC]: Independent Clause
(DC): Dependent Clause

Taming Nature

[The *story* of the American West **has been** a story of conquest.] **IC** While Americans were subjugating Native Americans, they were also taming a hostile nature. Because Americans have always wanted to tame nature, they have built dams, erected wind farms, dug tunnels, and mined for gold. Therefore, today Americans are too often not part of nature since they experience the latter only on the vacation trips to national or state parks. Nature becomes for them a retreat from the hectic pace of daily existence, where they rediscover themselves and their human spirit. This experience is separated and made distinct from daily life, in which the "natural" environment is often completely altered to fit human tastes. Indeed, the typical daily experience of nature for the average American of the city or the suburbia is through manicured lawns, planted flowers, and trees lining boulevards. Again, this daily experience is through a tamed natural environment; what this means is that once more Americans need to conquer nature.

Practice with Clauses

1. Identify all predicates by underlining them, and then identify their subjects by circling (here, in italics) them.

2. Identify all the clauses: a) mark the independent clauses with brackets [...] and **IC**; b) mark the dependent clauses with parentheses (...) and **DC**.

3. Make three separate columns: a) list all Adverb (Dependent) Clauses--*e.g.*; b) list all the Adjective (Dependent) Clauses—*e.g. people; c)*list all Noun (Dependent) Clauses—*e.g.*

4. On a separate sheet of paper, try to convert all dependent clauses in the passage into independent ones.

After they planted palm trees...

Dependent Clause

Freeways transform nature.

Independent Clause

WORDS OF DEPENDENCE

RELATIVE PRONOUNS

DEFINITION AND FORM	EXAMPLE
Relative pronouns introduce adjective dependent clauses that modify nouns and pronouns.	The *instructor* **who** assigned this exam is very demanding.
who, whoever, what, whatever, which, whichever, that, whom, whomever, whose	The *exam* **which (or that)** I took yesterday was very challenging.

***Relative pronouns should not be confused with interrogative pronouns of the same form. Always look at the function of the term in the specific context.

Who assigned this exam? *Interrogative pronoun introduces independent clause question.*

RELATIVE ADVERBS

DEFINITION AND FORM	EXAMPLE
Relative adverbs introduce adjective dependent clauses that modify nouns and pronouns.	The *year* **when** I was in Germany was full of new experiences.
when, where, whenever, wherever, why, how	The *country* **where** I always want to return is Germany.

***Relative adverbs should not be confused with the subordinating conjunctions of the same form (when, where, etc). Always look at the function of the term in the specific context.

When I was in Germany, I had many new experiences. *Subordinating conjunction introduces adverb dependent clause.*

SUBORDINATING CONJUNCTIONS

DEFINITION AND FORM	EXAMPLE

Subordinating conjunctions introduce adverb dependent clauses that modify other clauses. Notice how the meaning changes based on the particular subordinating conjunction used.

Time: after, before, once, since, until, when, whenever, while

After he spent a year abroad, he gained a different world view.

Condition: if, even if, provided that, unless

If you spend a year abroad, you will gain a different world view.

Contrast: although, even though, though, whereas

Although he spent a year abroad, he did not gain a different world view.

Location: wherever, where

Wherever he spent a year, he did not gain a different world view.

Choice: than, whether

Whether he spent a year abroad or in the country, he did not gain a different world view.

Cause/Effect: as, because, since

Because he spent a year abroad, he gained a different world view.

Result: so that, in order that, that

He spent a year abroad **so that** he could gain a different world view.

***Subordinating conjunctions should not be confused with prepositions of the same form. Always look at the function of the term in the specific context.

Since his year abroad he gained a different world view. *Prepositional phrase not a clause.*

Because of his year abroad, he gained a different world view. *Prepositional phrase not a clause.*

While abroad he gained a different world view. *Prepositional phrase not a clause.*

Chapter Three--Mini-Review: Clauses

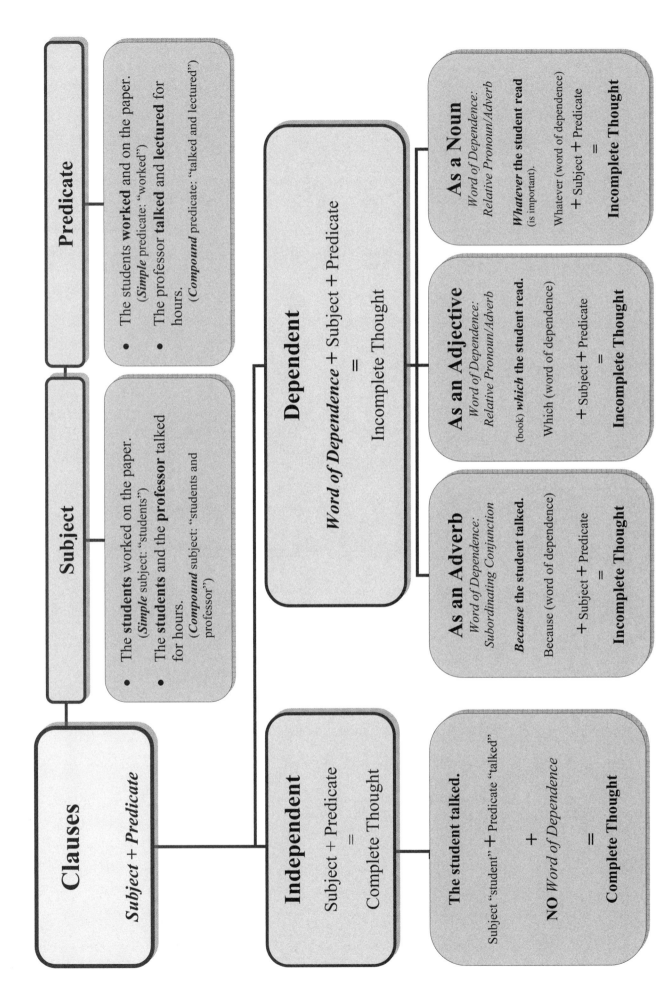

Clauses

Subject + Predicate

Subject

- The **students** worked on the paper. (*Simple* subject: "students")
- The **students** and the **professor** talked for hours. (*Compound* subject: "students and professor")

Predicate

- The students **worked** and on the paper. (*Simple* predicate: "worked")
- The professor **talked** and **lectured** for hours. (*Compound* predicate: "talked and lectured")

Independent

Subject + Predicate
=
Complete Thought

The student talked.
Subject "student" + Predicate "talked"
+
NO *Word of Dependence*
=
Complete Thought

Dependent

Word of Dependence + Subject + Predicate
=
Incomplete Thought

As an Adverb
Word of Dependence:
Subordinating Conjunction

Because the student talked.

Because (word of dependence)
+ Subject + Predicate
=
Incomplete Thought

As an Adjective
Word of Dependence:
Relative Pronoun/Adverb

(book) **which** the student read.

Which (word of dependence)
+ Subject + Predicate
=
Incomplete Thought

As a Noun
Word of Dependence:
Relative Pronoun/Adverb

Whatever the student read (is important).

Whatever (word of dependence)
+ Subject + Predicate
=
Incomplete Thought

SENTENCES

Formal Definition

Form: A sentence is a group of related words that must include **at least** one independent clause (i.e. one set of a subject and a predicate without a word that creates dependence). However, a sentence can include more than one clause as well as phrases.

Function: As a group of related words, a sentence conveys a complete meaning about a subject performing an action (predicate), about something (subject) happening (predicate), or about a subject in a certain state of being (predicate).

Etymology: The word *sentence* in Medieval English meant an aphorism, a brief statement of principle or opinion. With time, sentences became the main bearers of meaning (statements, opinions, principles, etc.)

Informal Definition

One can easily understand the importance of clauses and other units of meaning just by taking a look at nature. Nature constitutes a system of various units of life (meaning). One of those main units of life (meaning) is trees. As a complete unit of life (meaning), a tree consists of certain important parts, integral to its existence: roots, a trunk, branches, leaves, even blossoms. During the various seasons of the year, the tree may change shape and

form; it may discard its leaves or change their color, or it may blossom. Sentences (complete units of meaning) are like trees (complete units of life). Just like trees, sentences can adopt various forms to combine all kinds of elements such as clauses and phrases or even discard some. However, to be complete and to survive, sentences always need their "roots and trunk", their independent clauses.

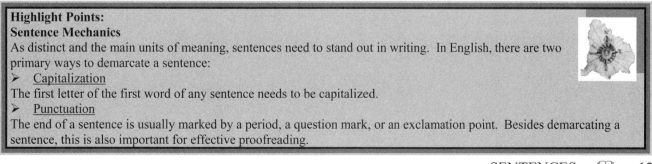

Highlight Points:
Sentence Mechanics
As distinct and the main units of meaning, sentences need to stand out in writing. In English, there are two primary ways to demarcate a sentence:
➢ Capitalization
The first letter of the first word of any sentence needs to be capitalized.
➢ Punctuation
The end of a sentence is usually marked by a period, a question mark, or an exclamation point. Besides demarcating a sentence, this is also important for effective proofreading.

SENTENCE PURPOSES

As units of meaning, sentences have different purposes. They can be used to make statements, to ask questions, to give commands, or to express strong feelings. There are four sentence purposes: **Declarative**, **Interrogative**, **Imperative**, and **Exclamatory**.

Declarative Sentences

Definition	Example
A declarative sentence is used to make a statement (declaration).	Environmentalists often participate in demonstrations.

Interrogative Sentences

Definition	Example
An interrogative sentence is used to ask a question (interrogation).	Do environmentalists often participate in demonstrations?

Imperative Sentences

Definition	Example
An imperative sentence is used to give a command (Latin: *imperare* meaning *to command*)	Protect the environment at all costs.

Exclamatory Sentences

Definition	Example
An exclamatory sentence is used to express strong feeling (exclaims at or about something).	How efficiently the demonstration was organized!

SENTENCE TYPES

Sentences are classified into different types according to their properties. These properties determine what kind of clauses the sentence consists of. There are four main types of sentences: **Simple, Compound, Complex,** and **Compound-Complex**. These types do not account for any phrases included; it is only clauses that affect the type of a sentence.

Note***: in the following examples Independent Clauses are marked as IC and with brackets, Dependent Clauses are marked as DC and with parentheses.

Simple Sentences

Definition	Example
A simple sentence consists of only one independent clause.	[Scientists observe nature.] *IC* *Independent Clause*

Highlight Points

A. Minimum Sentence Requirement

One independent clause is the minimum requirement for any correct sentence. If a sentence does not include at least one independent clause, then it is only a part of a sentence, a Fragment.

B. Fragments

Fragments are only parts of sentences. In form they do not have the requisite elements of a sentence that is at least one independent clause. In function they cannot form a complete unit of meaning. The following are the most common cases of fragments:

➤ Sentence with only Dependent Clause(s)

> ***After scientists reviewed the data***. *(Incorrect Sentence--Fragment)*
>
> *This is a dependent clause and both its form and its function (incomplete meaning) do not fulfill the requirements of a correct sentence. Therefore, a dependent clause that stands on its own without an independent clause to rely on is a fragment.*

➤ Sentence with only Phrase(s)

> ***After reviewing the data***. *(Incorrect Sentence--Fragment)*
>
> *This is a phrase and both its form and its function (incomplete meaning) do not fulfill the requirements of a correct sentence. Therefore, a phrase that stands on its own without an independent clause to rely on is a fragment.*

C. Correcting Fragments

In both of the above cases, all one needs to do is to create an independent clause within the sentence. There are multiple ways of doing so. The following are some of those ways:

➤ Delete words that create dependence:

> ~~*After*~~ *Scientists reviewed the data. (Correct Sentence--Fragment)*

> *This is now a correct sentence that consists of one independent clause that was created by taking out the word that created dependence (subordinating conjunction of time: After). This sentence has now the minimum requirement of one independent clause.*

➤ Add an Independent Clause:

> *After scientists reviewed the data,* ***they published the results****. (Correct Sentence)*

> *This is now a correct sentence that consists of one dependent clause and one independent clause that was added to support the dependent one. This sentence has now the minimum requirement of one independent clause.*

> *After reviewing the data,* ***the scientists published the results****. (Correct Sentence)*

This is now a correct sentence that consists of one phrase and one independent clause that was added to support the phrase. This sentence has now the minimum requirement of one independent clause.

Compound Sentences

Definition	Example

A compound sentence consists of two or more independent clauses without any dependent clauses. In a compound sentence, the independent clauses must be joined in one of the following ways:

- By a comma followed by a coordinating conjunction (**F**or, **A**nd, **N**or, **B**ut, **O**r, **Y**et, **S**o)

- By a comma followed by a correlative conjunction (neither/nor, either/or, etc.)

- By a semicolon (usually followed by a conjunctive adverb such as however, therefore, moreover, etc.)

[Scientists observe nature] *IC*, **and** [they record their findings.] *IC*

> *Independent Clause*
> *+ , Coordinating Conjunction*
> *+ Independent Clause*

[Scientists not only observe nature] *IC*, **but** [they also record their findings.] *IC*

> *Independent Clause*
> *+ , Correlative Conjunction*
> *+ Independent Clause*

[Scientists observe nature] *IC*; [**moreover,** they record their findings.] *IC*

> *Independent Clause*
> *+ ; (conjunctive adverb,)*
> *+ Independent Clause*

Highlight Points:

A. Commas

➢ Compound Sentences vs. Compound Predicates

When using a coordinating or correlative conjunction to connect two independent clauses, one always needs a comma before the conjunction.

When using a coordinating conjunction to connect two predicates, one does not need a comma before the conjunction.

[Scientists observe nature] *IC* ***,and*** *[they record their findings.]* *IC*

*[Scientists observe nature **and** record their findings.]* *IC* *(one IC with two predicates)*

B. Errors in Connecting Independent Clauses

➤ Comma Splice

In a compound sentence, independent clauses cannot be connected only by a comma. That creates a comma splice.

> *Scientists observe nature, they record their findings. (Incorrect connection of independent clauses- Comma Splice)*

➤ Run-On Sentence

In a compound sentence, independent clauses cannot be just placed next to each other without a conjunction or a semicolon. That creates a run-on sentence.

> *Scientists observe nature they record their findings. (Incorrect connection of independent clauses- Run-On)*

C. Correcting Connection Errors

➤ Correcting a Comma Splice

Add a coordinating, a correlative conjunction, or a semicolon (and usually a conjunctive adverb)

> *Scientists observe nature**, and** they record their findings.*

> *Scientists **not only** observe nature**, but** they **also** record their findings.*

> *Scientists observe nature**; (furthermore,)** they record their findings.*

➤ Correcting a Run-On Sentence

Add a comma and a coordinating, or a correlative conjunction, or a semicolon (and usually a conjunctive adverb) (see Comma Splice).

Complex Sentences

Definition	Example
A complex sentence consists of one independent clause and one or more dependent clauses.	**(When** scientists observe nature) *DC*, [they always record their findings.] *IC*

Highlight Points:

A. Comma Usage

In a complex sentence, the positioning of the clauses is important for comma usage.

➢ Independent Clause + (Adverb) Dependent Clause

If the IC precedes the Adverb DC, no comma is necessary between the two clauses.

[Scientists observe nature] **IC** *(because they need empirical data.)* **DC**

➢ (Adverb) Dependent Clause , + Independent Clause

If the Adverb DC precedes the IC, then a comma is always necessary between the two clauses.

(Because scientists need empirical data) **DC**, *[they observe nature.]IC*

➢ Independent Clause + Restrictive /Nonrestrictive (Adjective) Dependent Clause

If the Adjective DC is necessary (**restrictive**) for the meaning of the IC, then no comma(s) is necessary to separate it from the noun or pronoun it modifies.

*Scientists **who observe nature** need empirical data.*

If the Adjective DC is not absolutely necessary (**nonrestrictive**) for the meaning of the IC, then (a) comma(s) is necessary to separate it from the noun or pronoun it modifies. An adjective DC is not considered absolutely necessary when it just provides additional or explanatory information about the noun or pronoun that it modifies.

*Scientists, **who may come from all over the world**, observe nature for empirical data.*

B. Fragments

Dependent clauses cannot form a correct complete sentence. They always need the minimum requirement of one independent clause to rely on. Otherwise, they create parts of a complete sentence; they create fragments (for more, see Sentence Structures: Simple Sentences).

Compound-Complex Sentences

Definition	Example
A compound-complex sentence consists of two or more independent clauses and one or more dependent clauses. The independent clauses must be joined by a comma followed by a coordinating or correlative conjunction.	[Scientists observe nature] **IC, and** [they carefully record their findings] **IC** (**because** they need to publish accurate data.) **DC**

Travelogue

July 15th, 2005

Viva Las Vegas!

{(Even though it is a metropolis of over 1.5 million people,) DC [Las Vegas seems to lack a real reason to exist, for it is in the middle of the desert.]IC} (Compound-Complex)

{(Because in the summer the temperature seldom drops below 100 degrees,) DC [it makes for a quite challenging environment for humans.]IC} (Complex) {[However; once more, humans have tamed nature by harnessing the power of the Colorado river,]IC (which they managed through the building of nearby Hoover Dam.)DC (Complex) {[Indeed, the power generated by Hoover Dam not only powers the Las Vegas night sky,] IC [but it also makes this city livable through incessantly running air-conditioning units.]IC} (Compound)

{[This city, with its particularly famous Las Vegas Strip, is a manifestation of man's desire to conquer nature and is a testament to man's ingenuity.]}IC (Simple) {(Although Las Vegas is rather impressive,) DC [it can also be perceived as wasteful.]IC} (Complex)

[IC]: Independent Clause
(DC): Dependent Clause
{}: Sentence

One American Paradox

[*Americans* <u>have developed</u> a passion for their national parks.] **IC**- {*simple declarative sentence*} Over 277 million people visited the national park system in 2004, which doesn't include state and local reserve or park areas. Indeed, Americans eagerly leave their busy lives because they want to bare witness to the majesty of nature. The paradox then is that Americans spend their ten days of annual vacation in a national park in awe of this untouched nature. They then return home to areas like Las Vegas which represent the absolute subjugation and conquest of nature. On the way back from the Grand Canyon, one finds Las Vegas. This is a city of millions, and it was developed in a vast and arid desert although no resources were available there. Despite the intense heat and lack of water, houses boast lawns, hotels feature golf courses, air conditioners work at full power, and the famed strip of Las Vegas lights up the night sky for miles. Millions of light bulbs are powered through the once mighty Colorado River after it was tamed by the construction of Hoover Dam in the 1930s.

Practice with Sentences

1. Identify all predicates by underlining them, and then identify their subjects by circling (here, in italics) them.

2. Identify all the clauses: a) mark the independent clauses with brackets [...] and **IC**; b) mark the dependent clauses with parentheses (...) and **DC**.

3. On a sheet of paper, separate each sentence and characterize it according to its type (Simple, Compound, etc.).

4. On a sheet of paper, separate each sentence and characterize it according to its purpose (Declarative, Interrogative, etc.).

Paris has come to Las Vegas.

Simple Sentence

Chapter Three—Mini Review: Sentences

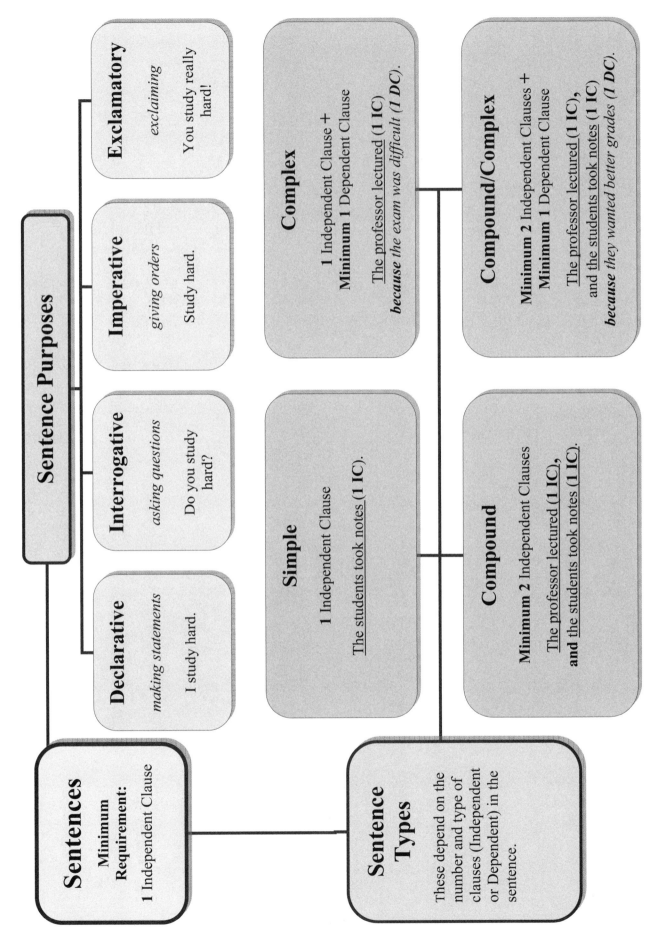

Sentences

Minimum Requirement: 1 Independent Clause

Sentence Purposes

Declarative

making statements

I study hard.

Interrogative

asking questions

Do you study hard?

Imperative

giving orders

Study hard.

Exclamatory

exclaiming

You study really hard!

Sentence Types

These depend on the number and type of clauses (Independent or Dependent) in the sentence.

Simple

1 Independent Clause

The students took notes (1 IC).

Complex

1 Independent Clause + Minimum 1 Dependent Clause

The professor lectured (1 IC) *because the exam was difficult (1 DC)*.

Compound

Minimum 2 Independent Clauses

The professor lectured (1 IC), **and** the students took notes (1 IC).

Compound/Complex

Minimum 2 Independent Clauses + Minimum 1 Dependent Clause

The professor lectured (1 IC), **and** the students took notes (1 IC) *because they wanted better grades (1 DC)*.

Chapter Three—Overview: Units of Meaning

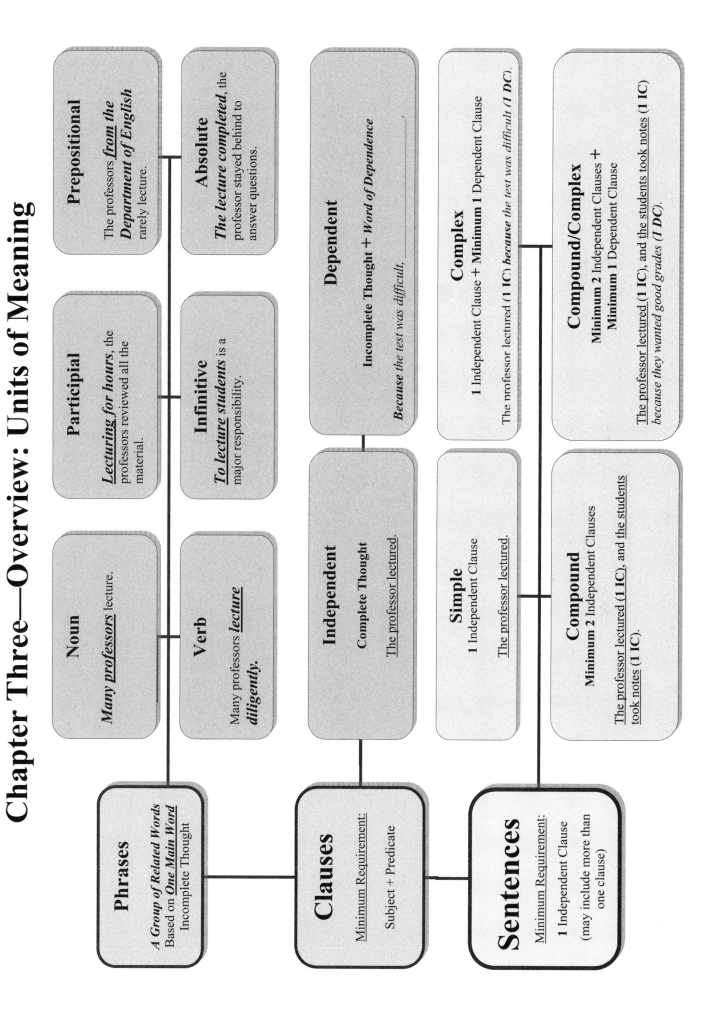

Prepositional

The professors *from the Department of English* rarely lecture.

Absolute

The lecture completed, the professor stayed behind to answer questions.

Participial

Lecturing for hours, the professors reviewed all the material.

Infinitive

To lecture students is a major responsibility.

Noun

Many professors lecture.

Verb

Many professors *lecture diligently.*

Phrases

A Group of Related Words Based on *One Main Word* Incomplete Thought

Dependent

Incomplete Thought + *Word of Dependence*

Because the test was difficult, _____

Independent

Complete Thought

The professor lectured.

Clauses

Minimum Requirement:

Subject + Predicate

Complex

1 Independent Clause + **Minimum 1 Dependent Clause**

The professor lectured (1 IC) *because the test was difficult (1 DC).*

Compound/Complex

Minimum 2 Independent Clauses + **Minimum 1 Dependent Clause**

The professor lectured (1 IC), and the students took notes (1 IC) *because they wanted good grades (1 DC).*

Simple

1 Independent Clause

The professor lectured.

Compound

Minimum 2 Independent Clauses

The professor lectured (1 IC), and the students took notes (1 IC).

Sentences

Minimum Requirement:

1 Independent Clause

(may include more than one clause)

Chapter 4
Agreement

In creating speech by bringing parts of speech and units of meaning together, one needs to be familiar with certain construction rules. In English, agreement is a category of such rules. Agreement regulates two construction issues: **Subject / Verb Agreement and Pronoun / Antecedent Agreement**. Indeed, subjects have to agree with their verbs in terms of number and person. Furthermore, pronouns have to agree with their antecedents, the words they replace or refer to, in terms of number, person, and gender. To construct meaning that is coherent and comprehensible to others, one needs to be familiar with and follow these rules of agreement.

Agreement

Rules of Construction

SUBJECT/VERB AGREEMENT:
General Principles

In every clause, the subject must agree with the verb in terms of number and person (for more on number and person, see Chapter 1: Noun/Pronoun/Verb Characteristics). A singular subject requires a verb in the singular, and a plural subject requires a verb in the plural. In English, there are various rules that control the agreement between subjects and verbs.

The following are some simple steps to ensure Subject/Verb Agreement:

STEP 1: Find the verb(s) of your clause

What is the action taking place? What is happening? What is the state of being?

Verbs are the words that show action, occurrence, or state of being. Furthermore, these words must be in a form that can function as a verb (for more, see Chapter 1: Verbs). Keep in mind that not all verb forms function as verbs in a sentence (e.g. infinitives).

Professors at universities <u>conduct</u> experiments to verify hypotheses.

The verb here is "conduct" because it shows action; also it is in the Base Form, so it can function as a verb. The words "to verify" could be mistaken for a verb because they also show action; however, they are in the Infinitive Form which can never function as a verb.

STEP 2: Find the subject(s) of your clause

Who/What is acting? Who/What is happening? Who/What is in the state of being?

Subjects show who/what acts, happens, or is in a certain state of being. Furthermore, subjects must be in a form that can function as such, more specifically in the subjective case (for more, see Chapter 1: Nouns: Noun Case, Chapter 2: Clauses: Subject). Keep in mind that nouns and pronouns can be subjects, objects, or owners depending on their case (subjective, objective, possessive). Therefore, it is important to distinguish form from function.

Professors at universities often <u>conduct</u> experiments with professors from other institutions.

After you find the verb "conduct," ask the question," Who conduct?"

The answer "Professors (conduct") gives you the subject of the verb. Notice there are two identical nouns "professors" in your sentence; only the first "professors" is in the subjective case and can function as a subject; the second "professors" is in the objective case and functions as the object of the preposition "with".

STEP 3: Make sure that the verb and its subject agree in number (singular or plural)

Is my verb singular or plural? How many are my subjects? Do they match?

Verbs and subjects must agree in number. Therefore, you need to know which subjects are singular or plural and how to form the singular and plural forms of verbs depending on the verb tense.

Professors at universities often <u>conduct</u> experiments with professors from other institutions.

The verb "conduct" is plural, and the subject "professors" is also plural (for more see Chapter 1: Nouns: Noun Number and Verbs: Verb Number).

STEP 4: Make sure that the verb and its pronoun subject agree in person (1st, 2nd, 3rd)

Person	Singular	Plural
1st	Am **I** the subject?	Are **we** the subject?
2nd	Are **you** the subject?	Are **you** the subject?
3rd	Is **he/she/it** the subject?	Are **they** the subject?

Verbs and subjects must agree in person. Therefore, you need to know what person your subject and verb are in.

They often <u>conduct</u> experiments with professors from other institutions. *The verb "conduct" is third person plural, and the subject "they" is also third person plural (for more see Chapter 1: Pronouns: Pronoun Person and Verbs: Verb Person).*

AGREEMENT RULES: SUBJECTS

There are a number of issues to consider when conjugating verbs and ensuring they match their subjects. These include locating the number/person, the subject/verb order in the sentence, the subject as compound or not, the subject(s) connected with conjunctions other than and, subjects with many modifiers, or subjects with subject complements.

NUMBER / PERSON

Definition	Example

The verb has to agree with its subject in terms of number: singular or plural and person: 1st, 2nd, or 3rd. The following is one of the most important rules:

Subject: 3rd person Singular

+

Verb: Simple Present Tense (–s Form) in the 3rd person singular

Person	Singular	Plural
1st	I conduct research.	We conduct research.
2nd	You conduct research.	You conduct research.
3rd	The professor/ (he/she/it) *conduct—s* research.	The professors/ (they) conduct research.

SUBJECT/VERB ORDER

Definition	Example

Rule: The subject of a verb is usually positioned before the verb.

Subject + Verb

Exceptions: Occasionally, the subject of a verb is positioned after the verb.

Verb + **Subject**

- With Questions
- With The structure : There is/ There are
- With some structures of emphasis

Students participate in experiments.

Do **students** participate in experiments?
In each experiment there are **problems.**
In this experiment there is one **problem.**
Had no **students** participated in the experiments, the latter would have failed.

COMPOUND SUBJECT

Definition	Example
Rule: A compound subject (two or more subjects connected with "and") is usually considered plural even if the individual subjects are singular. **1 Subject + and + 1 Subject** (or more) + <u>Verb</u> (in plural) **Exceptions**: Occasionally, a compound subject is considered singular when: • "each" or "every" modifies the compound subject. • two or more subjects refer to the same entity.	One **student and** one **professor** <u>participate</u> in this experiment. **Students, their advisors, and scientists** <u>participate</u> in experiments. **Each student and professor** <u>participates</u> in experiments. **The best professor and advisor** for students <u>is</u> Dr. Beehler.

SUBJECT WITH CONJUNCTIONS OTHER THAN "AND"

Definition	Example
Rule: When subjects are connected with conjunctions other than "and" (compound subject), the verb has to agree with the closest subject. ~~Subject 1+ Conjunction~~ + **Subject 2**+ <u>Verb</u>	~~The parents or~~ the **student** <u>has</u> to attend the orientation. ~~The student or~~ the **parents** <u>have</u> to attend the orientation. ~~Either the teaching assistants or~~ the **professor** <u>grades</u> the exams. ~~Neither the professor nor~~ his teaching **assistants** <u>grade</u> the exams. ~~Not only a high GPA but also~~ solid **letters** of recommendation <u>are</u> important.

*** This happens with conjunctions such as "or, nor, either…or, neither…nor, not only…but also" (for more see Chapter 1: Conjunctions). These conjunctions add subjects together, but for agreement purposes the above rule applies.

SUBJECT WITH MODIFIERS

Definition	Example
Rule: A subject is often accompanied by modifiers (adjectives, prepositional phrases, clauses). Ignore those modifiers in order to find the (simple or compound) subject.	A **major** ~~in the sciences~~ <u>is</u> very promising. ~~Good~~ **grades** ~~in history~~ <u>are</u> quite important. A ~~high~~ **GPA and** ~~solid~~ **letters** ~~of recommendation~~ <u>are</u> very important. (Compound Subject)

Subject (s) + ~~Modifiers~~ + Verb

*** Remember: any noun that is part of a prepositional phrase can never be the subject of a verb because it is the object of the preposition (for more see Chapter 1: Nouns: Case)

A ~~high~~ **GPA** ~~along with solid letters of recommendation~~ is very important. (Simple Subject)

***Keep in mind: along <u>with</u>, together <u>with</u>, as well <u>as</u>, accompanied <u>by</u>, in addition to may trick you to think your subject is compound; however, they are only prepositional phrases and should be ignored.

SUBJECT vs. SUBJECT COMPLEMENT

Definition	Example
<u>Rule</u>: A linking verb needs to agree with its subject not the subject complement. Just ignore the number of the subject complement. **Subject** + <u>Linking Verb</u> + ~~Subject Complement~~	An important **factor** in college success <u>is</u> ~~skilled instructors~~. **Researchers** <u>are</u> a ~~collaborative community~~.

SUBJECT/VERB AGREEMENT: NOUNS AS SUBJECTS

The following rules specifically apply to nouns as subjects. This means that all the previous rules also apply.

NON-COUNT NOUNS AS SUBJECTS

Definition	Example

<u>Rule</u>: Non-Count nouns as subjects can only be singular. Therefore, their verb has to be singular (for more see Chapter 1: Nouns: Noun Types).
    Subject (Non-Count Noun) = Always Singular
        + <u>Verb</u> (Always Singular)
	Coffee <u>is</u> necessary during exams. (Non-Count Noun: fluid)
	College **education** <u>requires</u> critical thinking. (Non-Count Noun: idea)
	Statistics <u>constitutes</u> a requirement for many majors. (Non-Count Noun: field of study)
	Competing often creates unnecessary stress. (Non-Count Noun: activity)

*** Remember: non-count nouns also include **nouns that end with an –s** but are singular such as physics, statistics, economics, mathematics (fields of study).

COLLECTIVE NOUNS AS SUBJECTS

Definition	Example

Rule: Collective nouns are count nouns that group similar persons, places, things, or ideas together in one unit. Therefore, these nouns can form both the singular and the plural, and their verb has to agree (for more see Chapter 1: Nouns: Noun Types).

This **team** <u>is</u> responsible for recycling.

These **teams** <u>are</u> responsible for recycling.

   Subject (Collective Count Noun) = Singular or Plural

+

   <u>Verb</u> (Singular or Plural)

Exception: Even if a collective noun is in the singular, as a subject it can sometimes take its verb in the plural. This happens when the members or parts of the group/unit function individually and not as one.

The environmental **committee** <u>makes</u> important decisions. (As one unit)

The environmental **committee** <u>have</u> to first take their seats. (As individuals)

SPECIAL NOUNS AS SUBJECTS

Definition	Example
Nouns such as amounts of time, money, distance, or measurement are considered singular.	**Two hours** <u>is</u> the time allotted for this exam. **Sixty dollars** <u>is</u> the fee for this exam. **Two miles** <u>is</u> the distance to the campus. **One thousand square feet** <u>is</u> the size of the lecture hall.
Nouns such as "athletics, ethics, news, measles, politics, the United States of America" are considered singular despite the –**s** at the end (all these nouns, except for the U.S., are non-count abstract nouns anyway).	The **news** about education <u>is</u> encouraging. **Politics** <u>is</u> a significant factor in making decisions.
Nouns such as "eyeglasses, clippers, jeans, pants, scissors, tweezers, thanks, riches" are considered plural even though they refer to one thing. However, if you use "pair" with "eyeglasses, clippers, jeans, pants, scissors, tweezers," then they are considered singular.	**Jeans** <u>are</u> the favorite student outfit. **A pair** of regular jeans <u>costs</u> forty dollars. Many **thanks** <u>are</u> owed to my advisor.
Nouns such as "means and series" can be either singular or plural depending on the context.	The **means** to an end <u>has</u> to be ethical. Several **means** of transportation <u>are</u> available.
Nouns such as plural titles of written works (or films) are considered singular.	*The Brothers Karamazov* <u>is</u> a novel by the Russian author Fyodor Dostoevsky.
Nouns such as plural company names are considered singular.	**Londer Brothers** <u>supplies</u> the university with paper.

SUBJECT/VERB AGREEMENT: PRONOUNS AS SUBJECTS

The following rules specifically apply to pronouns as subjects. However, all the previous rules apply.

RELATIVE PRONOUNS AS SUBJECTS
Who, Which, That

Definition	Example
When the subject of the verb is the relative pronoun "who, which, or that" the verb agrees with the pronoun's antecedent (the word the pronoun refers to). *Antecedent (Singular)* — **Subject** (Relative Pronoun) + Verb (**Singular**) *Antecedent (Plural)* – Subject (Relative Pronoun) + Verb (**Plural**)	The *instructor* **who** <u>teaches</u> this course is helpful. The *instructors* **who** <u>teach</u> this course are helpful. The *key* **which** <u>opens</u> this lab is lost. The *keys* **which** <u>open</u> this lab are lost.

***Remember: this rule does not apply to whom and whose; these are relative pronouns, but they are in the objective and possessive case accordingly. Therefore, they cannot be subjects.

INDEFINITE PRONOUNS AS SUBJECTS

Definition	Example

When the subject of the verb is an indefinite pronoun, you need to determine whether the pronoun is singular or plural (for more see Chapter 1: Pronouns: Pronoun Types).

Singular Indefinite Pronouns:
- all pronouns with "one" in them: one, someone, no one (or none), anyone, everyone
- all pronouns with "body" in them: somebody, nobody, anybody, everybody
- all pronouns with "thing" in them: something, nothing, anything, everything
- each, every
- either, neither
- another

Anyone <u>is</u> capable of passing such an easy test.
Somebody in this room <u>is trying</u> to cheat.

Nothing <u>impedes</u> motivated students from succeeding.
Each in this group <u>has</u> to be responsible for this project.

Neither of these tests <u>fulfills</u> the requirement.
Another of these forms <u>is</u> available online.

*** **None** is an indefinite pronoun that is ambiguous. Some consider **none** as always singular because it derives from "no one." Others argue that it can be either singular or plural depending on the context. This book follows the first theory.

Plural Indefinite Pronouns:

    both, many, few, several

Both <u>are</u> responsible for the final outcome.

Many <u>need</u> to collaborate for the final outcome.

Singular/Plural Indefinite Pronouns:

    all, more, some, most, any

All of the materials <u>are</u> to be handled carefully.

All of the toxic fluid <u>was</u> spilled on the floor.

Some of the courses <u>are</u> very interesting.

Some of the curriculum <u>is</u> rather repetitive.

***In these cases of singular or plural indefinite pronouns, you need to look at the context to determine the number of the pronoun/subject. If there is a prepositional phrase modifying the subject, take it into consideration, but remember: the object of the preposition cannot be the subject of your verb.

PRONOUN/ANTECEDENT AGREEMENT: GENERAL PRINCIPLES

SIX IMPORTANT STEPS

In English, pronouns are the words that replace or refer to nouns (sometimes other pronouns). Therefore, the number and person of each pronoun must agree with the noun it replaces or refers to (for more on number and person, see Chapter 1: Noun/Pronoun Characteristics). A singular noun (antecedent) should be connected to a singular pronoun. A plural noun (antecedent) should be connected to a plural pronoun. In both cases, the pronoun has to be in the right person (1st, 2nd, 3rd). In English, there are various rules that control the agreement between pronouns and their antecedents.

The following are some simple steps to ensure Pronoun/Antecedent Agreement:

STEP 1: Find the pronoun(s)

Pronouns are the words that replace or refer to nouns. There are various types of pronouns depending on their function in the specific context (for more see Chapter 1: Pronouns/ Pronoun Types).

Dr. Briggs is a professor at the university. **He** is the Director of the Basic Writing Program.

The pronoun here is "He". It is a personal pronoun in the 3rd person singular in the subjective case (subject of the verb "is").

STEP 2: Find the antecedent of your pronoun

Which noun does the pronoun replace? Whom/What does the pronoun refer to?

These are the words that show whom/what the specific pronoun replaces or refers to (for more, see Chapter 1: Pronouns).

<u>Dr. Briggs</u> is a professor at the university. **He** is the Director of the University Writing Program.

After you find the pronoun "He", ask the question, "Whom does 'he' replace/refer to?"

The answer "Dr. Briggs" gives you the antecedent of the pronoun.

STEP 3: Make sure that the pronoun and its antecedent agree in number (singular or plural)

Is the pronoun singular or plural? Is its antecedent singular or plural? Do they match?

Pronouns must agree with their antecedents in number. Therefore, you need to know which antecedents (nouns) are singular or plural and how to form the singular and plural forms of pronouns.

<u>Instructors</u> are usually available for questions during **their** office hours.

The antecedent "Instructors" is plural, and the pronoun "their" is also plural (for more see Chapter 1: Nouns/Pronouns: Noun/Pronoun Number).

STEP 4: Make sure that the pronoun and its antecedent agree in person (1st, 2nd, 3rd)

Pronouns and their antecedents must agree in terms of person. Therefore, you need to know what person the pronoun and the antecedent are in.

<u>Instructors</u> are usually available for questions during office hours. **They** often hold additional office hours during finals' week.

The antecedent "Instructors" is third person plural, and the pronoun "They" is also third person plural (for more see Chapter 1: Pronouns: Pronoun Person).

Person	Singular	Plural
1st	I, me, mine, my	we, us, ours, our
2nd	you, you, yours, your	you, you, yours, your
3rd	he, him, his, his/she, her, hers, her/it, it, its, its	they, them, theirs, their

***The above pronouns are only the personal pronouns, but they are the most commonly used ones. However, you need to keep in mind that there are other pronoun types to consider for pronoun/antecedent agreement.

STEP 5: Make sure that the pronoun and its antecedent agree in gender (female, male, neuter)

Is the antecedent female, male, or neuter?

Pronouns and their antecedents must agree in terms of gender. Therefore, you need to know the gender of the antecedent.

Mr. Thompson was accepted into the Master's program; **he** will be attending in Fall.

Mrs. Vance is determined to finish **her** dissertation in one year.

This lab has so many projects that the administration keeps **it** unlocked during most of the day.

In all of the above examples, the gender of the antecedent is clear, so the agreement is uncomplicated.

However, many times the gender of the antecedent is not clear. In those cases:

Use a singular female, male, or neuter pronoun if you are certain of the antecedent's gender.

The mail carrier delivered a package. **She** left it on the desk.

The antecedent "carrier" is third person singular, but it could be either male or female. Therefore, by using "she" you signify that you know the person's gender—because, for instance, you were there and saw her.

STEP 6: Make sure to avoid sexist language (only female or male pronouns)

How do you avoid sexist language?

If you are not certain of the antecedent's gender, try to avoid sexist language in one of the following ways:

- You can use pairs of pronouns: he/she, him/her, his/hers, his/her.
  An instructor has to be very focused on **his/her** students' needs.
  The antecedent instructor could be either female or male; therefore, you can use his/her as a pronoun.
- Using pairs of pronouns may be awkward. Use the plural for the antecedent and its pronoun.
  Instructors have to be very focused on **their** students' needs.
- You have to use pairs of pronouns for singular indefinite pronouns as antecedents: everyone, anyone, no one, etc. To avoid awkward constructions, you can also refashion the sentence without indefinite pronouns.
  Everyone enjoys having **his/her** work published in respectable journals. **OR**
  People/Scholars/Academics enjoy having **their** work published in respectable journals.

AGREEMENT RULES: PRONOUNS

There are a number of issues to consider when conjugating verbs and ensuring they match their subjects. These include locating the number/person, the subject/verb order in the sentence, the subject as compound or not, the subject(s) connected with conjunctions other than and, subjects with many modifiers, or subjects with subject complements.

COMPOUND ANTECEDENT

Definition	Example
Rule: A compound antecedent (two or more antecedents connected with "and") is usually considered plural even if the individual antecedents are singular. 1 Antecedent + and + 1 Antecedent (or more) = Plural → **Pronoun** (Plural) **Exceptions**: Occasionally, a compound subject is considered singular when: • "each" or "every" modifies the compound antecedent. • two or more antecedents refer to the same entity.	One student and an instructor discovered something fascinating when **they** conducted a new experiment. Some students, professors, and scientists claimed this research as **theirs**. Each experiment and project has **its** problems. Instructor and advisor, Dr. Strahan, is students' favorite teacher because of **her** patience and expertise.

ANTECEDENT WITH CONJUNCTIONS OTHER THAN "AND"

Definition	Example
Rule: When antecedents are connected with conjunctions other than "and" (compound subject), the pronoun has to agree with the closest antecedent. ~~Antecedent 1+ Conjunction~~ + Antecedent 2 (Singular) → **Pronoun** (Singular) ~~Antecedent 1+ Conjunction~~ + Antecedent 2 (Plural) → **Pronoun** (Plural)	~~Either the loudspeakers or~~ the remote control needs **its** batteries replaced. ~~Either the remote control or~~ the loudspeakers need **their** batteries replaced. ~~Neither the professor nor~~ the teaching assistants help **their** students. ~~Not only the committee members but also~~ the President voiced **his** opinion.

*** This happens with conjunctions such as "or, nor, either…or, neither…nor, not only…but also" (for more see Chapter 1: Conjunctions). These conjunctions add antecedents together, but for agreement purposes the above rule applies.

PRONOUN/ANTECEDENT AGREEMENT: NOUNS AS ANTECEDENTS

NON-COUNT NOUNS AS ANTECEDENTS

Definition	Example
Rule: Non-count nouns as antecedents are always singular. Therefore, the pronoun that replaces/refers to them has to be singular (for more see Chapter 1: Nouns: Noun Types). **Antecedent** (Non-Count Noun) = Always Singular → **Pronoun** (Always Singular)	Coffee is necessary during exams for **its** ingredients and properties. (Non-Count Noun: fluid) College education is challenging because **it** requires critical thinking. (Non-Count Noun: idea)

*** Remember: non-count nouns also include **nouns that end with an –s** but are singular such as physics, statistics, economics, mathematics (fields of study).

COLLECTIVE NOUNS AS ANTECEDENTS

Definition	Example
Rule: Collective nouns are count nouns that group similar persons, places, things, or ideas together in one unit. Therefore, these nouns can form both the singular and the plural, and the pronoun that replaces/refers to them has to agree (for more see Chapter 1: Nouns: Noun Types). **Subject** (Collective Count Noun) = Singular or Plural → **Pronoun** (Singular or Plural)	This team pays for **its** uniform. These teams pay for **their** uniforms.
Exception: Even if a collective noun is in the singular as an antecedent, the pronoun that replaces/refers to it may be in the plural. This happens when the members or parts of the group/unit can function individually and not as one.	The board announced **its** decision to the university senate. (As one unit) The board raised **their** hands to vote for a new regulation. (As individuals)

PRONOUN/ANTECEDENT AGREEMENT   149

PRONOUN/ANTECEDENT AGREEMENT: PRONOUNS AS ANTECEDENTS

INDEFINITE PRONOUNS AS ANTECEDENTS

Definition	Example

When the antecedent of a pronoun is an indefinite pronoun, you need to determine whether the pronoun is singular or plural (for more see Chapter 1: Pronouns: Pronoun Types) and (Chapter 4: Subject/Verb Agreement: Indefinite Pronoun Subjects)

Singular Indefinite Pronouns

If they refer to people (one, someone, anybody, etc)., they require a pair of pronouns (to avoid sexist language)

If they refer to things (something, anything, everything, etc.), they require a pronoun in neuter.

<u>Everyone</u> is free to express **his/her** opinion.

<u>Somebody</u> must have forgotten to turn **his/her** paper in.

Each in this group <u>has</u> to be responsible for this project.

<u>Neither</u> of these tests requires critical thinking; **it** just needs memorization.

<u>Another</u> of these computers had **its** monitor stolen.

*** **None** is an indefinite pronoun that is ambiguous. Some consider **none** as always singular because it derives from "no one." Others argue that it can be either singular or plural depending on the context. This book follows the first theory.

Plural Indefinite Pronouns require a pronoun in plural:

<u>Both</u> are responsible for **their** failure in the final.

<u>Many</u> need to bring **their** efforts together.

Singular/Plural Indefinite Pronouns require a pronoun in the singular or plural depending on their number in the specific context.

<u>All</u> of the *students* lost **their** interest after the first week.

<u>All</u> of the *campus* receives **its** power from solar panels.

***In these cases of singular or plural indefinite pronouns, you need to look at the context to determine the number of the pronoun/subject. If there is a prepositional phrase modifying the subject, you need to take it into consideration.

Chapter 5
Sentence Errors

In creating speech by combining parts of speech and units of meaning, one needs to be familiar with certain construction rules. In English, errors often occur during the construction of sentences. The major sentence errors are: **Fragments, Run-On, Comma Splice, Mixed Constructions, Misplaced Modifiers, and Dangling Modifiers**. To avoid these errors, one needs to know how to identify them and how to correct them. To construct meaning that is coherent and comprehensible to others, one needs to be familiar with and follow certain rules as well as develop a system for proofreading.

FRAGMENTS

FRAGMENT BASICS

With mixed constructions, you need to understand three main things:

A. Fragment Definition	What is a fragment? How does it affect meaning?
B. Fragment Identification	How can I find fragments in my writing?
C. Fragment Correction	How can I correct fragments?

FRAGMENT DEFINITION

What is a fragment?

A *fragment,* as the term implies, is only *a piece of a sentence* even though it appears to be a complete sentence. Because it starts with a capital letter and ends with a period (a question mark, an exclamation mark, or sometimes, a semi-colon), a fragment usually gives the impression of a complete sentence. However, a fragment is technically and essentially an error in sentence structure because it does not have the minimum requirement of *one independent clause*, so it cannot convey a complete thought (for more see Chapter 3: Sentence Structures: Sentences).

Fragment Examples

Helping John with grammar. *Who is helping John? This unit of meaning is only a participial phrase based on the main word helping. However, it does not convey a complete thought (no subject, no verb).*

His instructor helping John with grammar. *What about the instructor? You may know now who was helping John, but you are still missing a verb; "helping" is just a participle, so it can never function as a verb unless it is accompanied by a helping verb like "is, was, has been, etc."*

Because his instructor was helping John with grammar. *So, what happened because of the instructor's help? You may know now that the instructor was helping John with grammar, so you have a clause (a subject: **instructor** and verb: **was helping**); however, this clause is dependent, and it describes the cause of something. What is the effect? What happened because of the instructor's help? That you still don't know because your sentence is only a fragment of a complete thought.*

FRAGMENT IDENTIFICATION

All of the above sentences are only fragments, pieces of a sentence. To be able to correct these errors, you need to have a system. The following steps can help you develop this proofreading system to avoid and correct fragments and build correct sentences that convey complete thoughts:

STEP 1: Find and isolate each sentence in your writing.

How can you find and isolate each sentence in your writing?

In writing, sentences are found between periods, question marks, exclamation marks (and sometimes semi-colons). Also, ordinarily, the first letter of each sentence is capitalized. When you edit, try to find and isolate each sentence from the rest by putting it in brackets. Here you have one example sentence.

[Because his instructor was helping John with grammar.]

STEP 2: Find and identify the clause(s) in each sentence.

Does your sentence contain any clauses (sets of subjects and predicates)? If so, What are your clauses: dependent or independent? If not, does your sentence only have phrases?

The main rule for avoiding sentence fragments is that each sentence should have a minimum of *one independent clause*. Therefore, you need to make sure each sentence has this minimum requirement. To make this process easier, find the verb(s), their subject(s), and any word that creates dependence (Chapter 4: Agreement and Chapter 3: Sentence Structures). Mark your clauses with parentheses and DC for dependent and IC for independent.

[DC (Because the instructor was helping him with grammar.)]

*This sentence has one clause (verb: **was helping**, subject: **the instructor**. Additionally, this clause is introduced by the subordinating conjunction: **because**, so it is a dependent clause and cannot convey a complete thought.*

[phrase (Helping John with grammar.)]

This sentence does not even have a set of a subject and a verb (clause); it is only a participial phrase. Therefore, this unit of meaning is a fragment and cannot convey a complete thought.

STEP 3: Diagnose any fragment errors.

Does your sentence have the minimum requirement of one independent clause?

YES: If your sentence *does have the minimum requirement of one independent clause*, then *it is not a fragment*. You can now proceed to other editing issues.

NO: If your sentence *does not have the minimum requirement of one independent clause*, then *it is a fragment*. After you determine that your sentence is a fragment, you need to correct it.

FRAGMENT CORRECTION

To correct any fragment, you need to remember the basic rule: each sentence (the unit of meaning between two periods, semi-colons, question marks, or exclamation marks) needs to have at least *one independent clause*.

Fragments can come in many shapes and forms, but the following are the most common fragments. All other variations of fragments are based on these ones, so you can follow the same steps in correcting them.

TYPE 1: Sentence with only dependent clause(s)

How do you correct this fragment type?

> **[DC (Because his instructor was helping John with grammar.)]**

- *Delete words that create dependence:*

> **[IC (~~Because~~ h His instructor was helping John with grammar.)]**

This is now a sentence that has the minimum requirement of one independent clause, so it conveys a complete thought.

- *Add an independent clause:*

> **[DC (Because his instructor was helping John with grammar,) IC (John's writing improved.)]**

This is now a sentence that has the minimum requirement of one independent clause, so it conveys a complete thought.

TYPE 2: Sentence with only phrase(s)

How do you correct this fragment type?

[phrase (Helping John with grammar.)]

- *Turn the phrase into a complete independent clause by adding a subject and/or a verb:*

[IC (**The instructor was** helping John with grammar.)]

This is now a sentence that has the minimum requirement of one independent clause, so it conveys a complete thought.

- *Add an independent clause to the phrase:*

[IC (**Helping John with grammar, the instructor managed to improve John's writing.**)]

This is now a sentence that has the minimum requirement of one independent clause, so it conveys a complete thought.

TYPE 3: Phrases with lists and examples

How do you correct this fragment type?

[IC (**The instructor helped John with various grammar issues.**) phrase (**Fragments, comma splices, and run-ons.**)] **OR**

[IC (**The instructor helped John with various grammar issues.**) phrase (**For example, fragments, comma splices, and run-ons.**)]

This fragment type is no different than TYPE 2, but it is very common to be treated as a separate one. Again, however, the correction process is the same.

- *Turn the phrase into a complete independent clause by adding a subject and/or a verb:*

[IC (**Some of these errors were fragments, comma splices, and run-ons.**)] **OR**

[IC (**Some of these errors were, for example, fragments, comma splices, and run-ons.**)]

This is now a sentence that has the minimum requirement of one independent clause, so it conveys a complete thought.

- ***Add an independent clause to the phrase*** *(usually by connecting the list or example phrase to the preceding independent clause)*:

  [IC (The instructor helped John with various grammar issues: fragments, comma splices, and run-ons.)] *(Attention: A colon, not a semi-colon, can be used to introduce a list of elements.)* **OR**

  [IC (The instructor helped John with various grammar issues, for example, fragments, comma splices, and run-ons.)]

This is now a sentence that has the minimum requirement of one independent clause, so it conveys a complete thought.

RUN ON & COMMA SPLICE

RUN-ON & COMMA-SPLICE BASICS

With a run-on or a comma splice, you need to understand three main things:

A. **Run-On & Comma-Splice Definition**	What are these errors? How do they affect meaning?
B. **Run-On & Comma-Splice Identification**	How can I find these errors in my writing?
C. **Run-On & Comma-Splice Correction**	How can I correct these errors?

RUN-ON & COMMA-SPLICE DEFINITIONS

What is a run-on? & What is a comma splice?

A *run-on*, as the term implies, is *an error of two (or more) independent clauses running into each other* without any connection. However, independent clauses have to be connected with coordinating conjunctions, correlative conjunctions, a semi-colon (and a conjunctive adverb), or they have to be separated with a period (a question mark, an exclamation mark, and occasionally a semi-colon) (for more see Chapter 1: Parts of Speech: Conjunctions).

A *comma splice*, as the term implies, is *a connection with a comma* between two (or more) independent clauses. However, independent clauses can only be connected with coordinating conjunctions or correlative conjunctions, or they can be separated with a period (a question mark, an exclamation mark, and occasionally a semi-colon —and a conjunctive adverb). A comma is not an adequate connection (for more see Chapter 1: Parts of Speech: Conjunctions).

Both these errors have to do with connecting independent clauses, and they both require a minimum of two independent clauses in order to occur.

Run-On & Comma-Splice Examples

Martha is a great writer she can be an inspiring teacher of writing. *This sentence consists of two independent clauses and conveys two complete thoughts. However, the sentences (and thoughts) are not connected properly. They are just put next to each other without any connection, which causes them to run on each other. Therefore, this unit of meaning (sentence) is weak and gives the impression that the writer lacks clarity of thought.*

Martha is a great writer, she can be an inspiring teacher of writing. *As you can observe, a comma splice is nothing more than **a run-on with a comma**. Instead of no connection, the two (or more) independent clauses of a sentence are connected with only a comma. However, the sentences (and complete thoughts) are not connected properly. They are just put next to each other with only a comma as their connection. Therefore, this unit of meaning (sentence) is weak and gives the impression that the writer lacks clarity of thought.*

RUN-ON & COMMA-SPLICE IDENTIFICATION

All of the above sentences can convey complete thoughts because they include independent clauses in their structure. However, they do so in a way that confuses the reader. To be able to correct these errors, you need to have a system. The following steps can help you develop this proofreading system to avoid and correct run-on and comma-splice errors, and build correct sentences that convey complete and complex thoughts.

STEP 1: Find and isolate each sentence in your writing.

How can you find and isolate each sentence in your writing?

In writing, sentences are found between periods, question marks, exclamation marks (and sometimes semi-colons). Also, ordinarily, the first letter of each sentence is capitalized. When you edit, try to find and isolate each sentence from the rest by putting it in brackets. In both of the cases below, you have one sentence:

[Martha is a great writer she can be an inspiring teacher of writing.]

[Martha is a great writer, she can be an inspiring teacher of writing.]

STEP 2: Find and identify the clause(s) in each sentence.

Does your sentence contain any clauses (sets of subjects and predicates)? If so, What are your clauses: dependent or independent?

When editing, the main condition for checking whether there is a comma splice or a run-on is that a sentence should have a minimum of *two independent clauses*. If not, then there is no way there can be an error of a comma splice or a run-on. Therefore, you need to find the clauses in each sentence and identify them as dependent or independent. To make this process easier, find the verb(s), their subject(s), and any word that creates dependence (for more see Chapter 4: Agreement and Chapter 3: Sentence Structures). Mark your clauses with parentheses and DC for dependent and IC for independent.

> **[IC** (Martha is a great writer) **IC** (she can be an inspiring teacher of writing.)**]**

> **[IC** (Martha is a great writer), **IC** (she can be an inspiring teacher of writing.)**]**

*This sentence has two clauses (verbs: **is** and **is**, subjects: **Martha** and **she** accordingly). These clauses are both independent because neither includes a word that creates dependence, and both convey complete thoughts (for more see Chapter 3: Sentence Structures: Clauses).*

STEP 3: Diagnose any run-on or comma-splice errors.

What is the connection between the two (or more) independent clauses of your sentence?

A coordinating conjunction, a correlative conjunction (or a semi-colon and a conjunctive adverb): If the two (or more) independent clauses in your sentence are connected with a coordinating conjunction or a correlative conjunction, *your sentence **does not have the error of a run-on or a comma splice**.* You can now proceed to other editing issues.

No connection or a comma connection: If the two (or more) independent clauses in your sentence are connected with nothing or with only a comma, then your sentence **has the error of a run-on or a comma splice** accordingly. After you determine that your sentence has these errors, you need to correct them.

RUN-ON & COMMA-SPLICE CORRECTION

To correct any run-on or comma-splice error, you need to remember the basic rule: to connect independent clauses, you need a coordinating conjunction or a correlative conjunction. However, you have additional options in order to correct these errors.

The following are the options you have in correcting a run on or a comma splice.

Option 1: Connect the independent clauses properly.

How do you properly connect two (or more) independent clauses?

> *Run On*: [IC (Martha is a great writer) IC (she can be an inspiring teacher of writing.)]

> *Comma Splice*: [IC (Martha is a great writer), IC (she can be an inspiring teacher of writing.)]

- *__With a coordinating conjunction (FANBOYS: for, and, nor, but, or, yet, so) and a comma:__*

  [IC (Martha is a great writer) IC (, *and* she can be an inspiring teacher of writing.)]

- *__With a correlative conjunction (not only … but also, either … or, neither … nor, etc.):__*

  [IC (*Not only* is Martha a great writer) IC (, *but* she can *also* be an inspiring teacher of writing.)]

Option 2: Separate the independent clauses properly.

How do you properly separate two (or more) independent clauses?

> *Run On*: [IC (Martha is a great writer) IC (she is an inspiring teacher of writing.)]

> *Comma Splice*: [IC (Martha is a great writer), IC (she can be an inspiring teacher of writing.)]

- *__With a period, a question mark, or an exclamation mark (not with a comma):__*

  [IC (Martha is a great writer.)] [IC (Sshe can be an inspiring teacher of writing.)]

- *__With a semi-colon and a conjunctive adverb (furthermore, however, moreover, etc.):__*

  [IC (Martha is a great writer) IC (; *furthermore,* she can be an inspiring teacher of writing.)]

Option 3: Turn one independent clause to a dependent clause.

How do you properly turn an independent clause to a dependent clause?

>   *Run On*: [IC (Martha is a great writer) IC (she can be an inspiring teacher of writing.)]

>   *Comma Splice:* [IC (Martha is a great writer), IC (she can be an inspiring teacher of writing.)]

*   <u>*By adding a word that creates dependence (relative pronoun/adverb, subordinating conjunction)*</u>:

    [DC (*Because* Martha is a great writer), IC (she is an inspiring teacher of writing.)]

    [DC (*Since* Martha is a great writer,) IC (she is an inspiring teacher of writing.)]

    [IC (Martha is such a great writer) DC (*that* she is an inspiring teacher of writing.)]

    [IC (Martha, DC (*who* is a great writer,) is an inspiring teacher of writing.)]

MIXED CONSTRUCTION

MIXED-CONSTRUCTION BASICS

With mixed constructions, as with most grammar errors, you need to understand three main things:

A. Mixed-Construction Definition	What is a mixed construction? How does it affect meaning?
B. Mixed-Construction Identification	How can I find a mixed construction in my writing?
C. Mixed-Construction Correction	How can I correct a mixed construction?

MIXED-CONSTRUCTION DEFINITION

What is a mixed construction?

As the term implies, a *mixed construction* is a sentence structure that consists of two or more incompatible parts. Those incompatible parts mix up the structure and confuse the reader. Usually mixed constructions occur when the writer starts a sentence with a certain thought in mind and half-way through, the writer comes up with another thought. That shift creates a mix up and confusion, which technically translates into the grammatical error of a mixed construction.

Mixed-Construction Examples

In the article by the psychologist argues against television. *This sentence starts out in the direction of explaining the content of an article. Suddenly, however, the writer starts talking about the psychologist who argues against television. Who "argues"? Obviously, the psychologist argues. However, the word "psychologist" cannot argue (be the subject of the verb) because it is the object of the prepositional phrase "by the psychologist." An object can never be a subject in the same sentence.*

Although the psychologist may be right does not make television absolutely worthless. *This sentence starts out with a dependent clause that expresses contrast, but the dependent clause (Although the psychologist may be right) is mixed with the independent clause's verb (does not make). Keep in mind that this error can also be viewed as a fragment given that the sentence lacks an independent clause (no subject for the second verb).*

MIXED-CONSTRUCTION IDENTIFICATION

All of the above sentences are mixed constructions because of the incompatible parts they consist of. These parts are mixed with each other creating confusion. To be able to correct mixed-construction errors, you need to have a system. In many ways, mixed constructions are similar to fragments, so you need to follow some of the same steps in identifying and correcting them. The following steps can help you develop this proofreading system to avoid and correct mixed constructions:

STEP 1: Find and isolate each sentence in your writing.

How can you find and isolate each sentence in your writing?

In writing, sentences are found between periods, question marks, exclamation marks (and sometimes semi-colons). Also, ordinarily, the first letter of each sentence is capitalized. When you edit, try to find and isolate each sentence from the rest by putting it in brackets. Here you have one sentence.

[In the article by the psychologist argues against television.]

STEP 2: Find and identify the clause(s) in each sentence.

Does your sentence contain any clauses (sets of subjects and predicates)? If so, look at the subject of each verb and make sure it is a noun, a pronoun, or their equivalents in the subjective case.

Often a mixed construction is the result of mixing up subjects and objects or using words that can never be subjects as such. Also, many mixed constructions could also be described as a fragment because as sentences they lack the minimum requirement of ***one independent clause although usually a mixed construction*** tricks you into believing otherwise.

In the article by the <u>psychologist</u> argues against television.

*This sentence consists of parts that make it appear like an independent clause (verb: **argues**, subject: (by) **the psychologist**.) However, upon closer observation, you can notice that this is not true. The supposed subject of the verb is not really its subject; instead, the word "psychologist" is the object of the preposition "by," so it cannot function as the subject of the verb. The writer here meant to have the object of the preposition also as the subject of the verb in the independent clause. However, that is not possible: a word can never be both an object and a subject at the same time; it can be either an object or a subject. Because the two parts, the prepositional phrase and the incomplete independent clause are mixed, this is a mixed construction.*

[DC (Although the psychologist may be right) does not make television worthless.]

This sentence also consists of parts that make it appear like it has an independent clause. However, upon closer observation, you can notice that this is not true. This sentence consists of a complete dependent clause (Although the psychologist may be right) and part of an independent clause (does not make television absolutely worthless). The writer here meant to have the dependent clause as the subject of the verb in the independent clause. However, that is not possible with adverb dependent clauses (for more, see Chapter 3: Sentence Structures: Clauses). Adverb clauses can never function as nouns (therefore, subjects and objects). Only noun dependent clauses can. Because the two parts of this sentence, the adverb dependent clause and the incomplete independent clause are mixed, this is a mixed construction.

STEP 3: Diagnose any mixed-construction errors.

Is the subject of a verb part (the object) of a prepositional phrase?

YES: If your sentence *does have part of a prepositional phrase as subject of a verb*, then your sentence contains *a mixed construction.*

Is the subject of a verb an adverb dependent clause?

YES: If your sentence *does have an adverb dependent clause as subject of a verb*, then your sentence contains *a mixed construction.*

MIXED-CONSTRUCTION CORRECTION

To correct any mixed construction, you need to remember that:

Mixed Constructions can come in many shapes and forms, but the following are the most common cases. All other variations of mixed constructions are based on these ones, so you can follow the same steps in correcting them.

In the article by the psychologist argues against television.

Although the psychologist may be right does not make television absolutely worthless.

How do you correct this mixed-construction type?

> In the article by <u>the psychologist</u> argues against television.

- *Take the word of dual function (subject and object) out of the prepositional phrase:*

In the article ~~by~~ the psychologist argues against television.

Now the word "psychologist" is no longer the object of the preposition "by" but only the subject of the verb "argues."

- *Add a subject for the verb that does not have one:*

In the article by the psychologist, <u>he</u> argues against television.

Now the verb "argues" has its own subject which is not the object of a preposition.

TYPE 2: When the subject of a verb is an adverb dependent clause.

How do you correct this mixed-construction type?

> Although the psychologist may be right does not make television worthless.

- *Convert the adverb dependent clause into a noun dependent clause:*

That ~~Although~~ the psychologist may be right does not make television worthless.

Now the subject of the verb "does not make" is no longer an adverb dependent clause, but a noun clause that can function as a subject.

- *Add a subject for the verb that does not have one (or has the adverb clause as its subject):*

Although the psychologist may be right, <u>this</u> does not make television worthless.

Now the verb "does not make" has its own subject which is not an adverb dependent clause but the pronoun, "this," which can function as a subject.

MISPLACED MODIFIER

MISPLACED-MODIFIER BASICS

With misplaced modifiers, as with most grammar errors, you need to understand three main things:

A. Misplaced-Modifier Definition	What is a misplaced modifier? How does it affect meaning?
B. Misplaced-Modifier Identification	How can I find a misplaced modifier in my writing?
C. Misplaced-Modifier Correction	How can I correct a misplaced modifier?

MISPLACED-MODIFIER DEFINITION

What is a misplaced modifier?

A modifier is a word or group of words that modifies (describes or limits) another word or group of words. As the term implies, a *misplaced modifier* is one that is in the wrong place creating confusion for the reader.

Misplaced-Modifier Examples

The student being helped <u>systematically</u> improved. *What happened systematically? Was the student being helped systematically, or did the student improve systematically? Obviously the modifier here is the adverb "systematically," but its positioning in the sentences creates confusion.*

This student was <u>only</u> taking notes. OR <u>Only</u> this student was talking notes. *Consider how the different positioning of the modifier "only" changes the meaning of this sentence.*

The instructor, <u>after having explained the concept</u>, <u>which was quite complex</u>, gave a quiz. *The positioning of the two modifiers here disrupts the continuity between subject and verb. The same is true for separating the verb from its object with too many modifiers.*

It is <u>a great, green, grammar</u> book. *The positioning of the modifiers that describes the book is incorrect. In English more than one adjective describing the same word are placed in a specific order.*

MISPLACED-MODIFIER IDENTIFICATION & CORRECTION

All of the above sentences create confusion because of the positioning of modifiers. To be able to correct these errors, you need to have a system. You need to realize that there are four most common cases of misplaced modifiers. Therefore, being aware of these cases can help you with their correction:

CASE 1: Avoid squinting modifiers.

How can you locate squinting modifiers?

As the term implies, these are the words that make you squint because you don't know what they are referring to exactly. They are usually positioned between two words, and they could be modifying both of them.

> **The student being helped <u>systematically</u> improved.**

How can you correct a squinting modifier?

Make sure each modifier refers to only one element in your sentence.

> **The student being helped improved <u>systematically</u>. OR**

> **Being <u>systematically</u> helped, the student improved.**

CASE 2: Be careful with limiting words.

What are limiting words?

As the term implies, these are the words that limit the meaning of the elements they modify. They are usually adverbs, most common of which are: only, not only, just, not just, almost, hardly, nearly, even, exactly, merely, scarcely, and simply.

> **This student was <u>only</u> taking notes.**

How can you place limiting words correctly?

Make sure the limiting word is placed only before the element it modifies; if placed elsewhere, it may alter the meaning of your sentence.

> **This student was <u>only</u> taking notes.**
> **<u>Only</u> this student was taking notes.**
> **This student was taking <u>only</u> notes.**

CASE 3: Avoid splits caused by modifiers.

How do modifiers cause splits?

In English the subject is usually close to the verb, and so is the object. Any words that come in between the subject and its verb or the verb and its object should not be too many and disrupt the continuity between those elements. An exception would be with adjective dependent clauses that need to be as close to the word they modify as possible. Also, short modifiers such as adverbs of frequency (often, usually, etc.) are often placed between the subject and its verb for emphasis.

The instructor, <u>after having explained the concept,</u> <u>which was quite complex,</u> gave a quiz.

How can you avoid such splits?

Make sure there are no long modifiers between the subject and the verb or the verb and the object.

<u>After having explained the concept,</u> <u>which was quite complex,</u> the instructor gave a quiz.

OR <u>After having explained the quite complex concept,</u> the instructor gave a quiz.

CASE 4: Arrange a string of adjectives correctly.

What is a string of adjectives?

In English it is common that you have more than one adjective modifying the same noun. In this case you need to arrange adjectives in a specific way. Many times errors occur in the placement of a string of adjectives.

It is <u>a great, green, grammar</u> book.

How can you arrange adjectives correctly?

The correct order for adjectives is:

1. **Determiner** (a, the, this, that, all, many, etc.)
2. **Opinion** (great, fascinating, terrible, etc.)
3. **Size or Shape** (big, small, tiny, square, oblong, rectangular, etc.)
4. **Color** (green, yellow, red, blue, etc.)
5. **Origin** (German, English, Chinese, Korean, Mexican, etc.)
6. **Material** (wooden, paper, steel, etc.)
7. **Noun used as adjective** (class, college, mother, etc.)

It is <u>a$^{(1)}$ great$^{(2)}$, green$^{(4)}$, grammar$^{(7)}$</u> book.

DANGLING MODIFIER

With dangling modifiers, as with most grammar errors, you need to understand three main things:

A. Dangling-Modifier Definition	What is a dangling modifier? How does it affect meaning?
B. Dangling-Modifier Identification	How can I find a dangling modifier in my writing?
C. Dangling-Modifier Correction	How can I correct a dangling modifier?

DANGLING-MODIFIER DEFINITION

What is a dangling modifier?

A modifier is a word or group of words that modifies (describes or limits) another word or group of words. As the term implies, a *dangling modifier* is one that only hangs loosely from a sentence without modifying any element in the sentence. Although these modifiers imply something as their object of description, that element cannot be found in the sentence. Instead, what they end up doing in the sentence is to modify the wrong or irrelevant element.

Dangling-Modifier Examples

<u>To encourage students excel</u>, **grades were not curved.** *Who encouraged students to excel? The grades? This is what this sentence is saying; however, what the writer probably meant is that the instructor encouraged the students to excel by not curving grades.*

<u>Creating challenging assignments</u>, **the students responded with enthusiasm.** *Who was creating challenging assignments? The students? This is what this sentence is saying; however, what the writer probably meant is that an instructor was responsible for these challenging assignments.*

<u>After grading all the papers</u>, **extensive feedback was given to students.** *Who graded the papers? The extensive feedback? This is what this sentence is saying; however, what the writer probably meant is that the instructor graded all the papers and then gave extensive feedback to students.*

DANGLING-MODIFIER IDENTIFICATION & CORRECTION

All of the above sentences include a dangling modifier. To be able to correct these errors, you need to have a system. You need to realize that there are three most common cases of dangling modifiers. Most of the times the dangling modifier is placed in the beginning of a sentence. Being aware of these cases can help you with their correction:

CASE 1: Dangling Modifiers with Infinitive Phrases

How can you locate a dangling modifier caused by an infinitive phrase?

These modifiers consist of an infinitive phrase positioned before a clause (for more see Chapter 3: Sentence Structures: Phrases). This infinitive phrase is supposed to modify a word that does not appear in the sentence but is just implied; instead, what this phrase does is to modify the subject of the clause which is irrelevant. The result is confusion.

> **<u>To encourage students to excel</u>, *grades* were not curved.**

Here, the modifier (underlined, infinitive phrase) appears to modify the word "grades." However, that does not make any sense because grades cannot encourage.

How can you correct a dangling modifier with an infinitive phrase?

Make sure you include the word that the modifier is really referring to. Oftentimes, like in this case, this dangling modifier is caused by the wrong use of passive voice, so you can convert your sentence to active voice.

> **<u>To encourage students to excel</u>, the instructor did not curve grades.**

CASE 2: Dangling Modifiers with Participial Phrases

How can you locate a dangling modifier caused by a participial phrase?

These modifiers consist of a participial phrase positioned before a clause (for more see Chapter 3: Sentence Structures: Phrases). This participial phrase is supposed to modify a word that does not appear in the sentence but is just implied; instead, what this phrase does is to modify the subject of the clause, which is irrelevant. The result is confusion.

> **<u>Creating challenging assignments</u>, *the students* responded with enthusiasm.**

Here, the modifier (underlined, participial phrase) appears to modify the word "students." However, that does not make any sense because probably the students were not the ones to create the assignments.

How can you correct a dangling modifier with a participial phrase?

Make sure you include the word that the modifier is really referring to.

> **<u>Although the instructor created challenging assignments</u>,** *the students* responded with enthusiasm.

CASE 3: Dangling Modifiers with Prepositional Phrases

How can you locate a dangling modifier caused by a prepositional phrase?

These modifiers consist of a prepositional phrase positioned before a clause (for more see Chapter 3: Sentence Structures: Phrases). This prepositional phrase is supposed to modify a word that does not appear in the sentence but is just implied; instead, what this phrase does is to modify the subject of the clause which is irrelevant. The result is confusion.

> **<u>After grading all the papers</u>, extensive feedback was given to students.**

Here, the modifier (underlined, prepositional phrase) appears to modify the word "feedback." However, that does not make any sense because feedback cannot grade papers.

How can you correct a dangling modifier with a prepositional phrase?

Make sure you include the word that the modifier is really referring to. Oftentimes, like in this case, this dangling modifier is caused by the wrong use of passive voice, so you can convert your sentence to active voice.

> **<u>After grading all the papers</u>,** *the instructor* gave extensive feedback to students.

Forming Noun Case and Number

A. Complete the table below with the appropriate forms of the possessive case, if applicable.

B. Add an appropriate noun to each of the nouns (owners) in the possessive case.

C. Make a sentence for each one of the sets of nouns you have created.

Noun	Possessive Singular	Possessive Plural	Sentence
1. country	*country's*	*countries'*	*A country's treasures are open to the inquisitive visitor. (Or The treasures of a country...)*
			Countries' treasures are open to the inquisitive visitor. (Or The treasures of countries...)
2. bus			
3. box			
4. compass			
5. group			
6. guest and host			
7. guide			
8. life			
9. today			
10. tour			

Identifying Regular and Irregular Plurals

Complete each sentence with the appropriate plural form of the noun in the parenthesis.

When traveling, it is always interesting to meet and socialize with the local *people* (person). Indeed, it is the _____ (people) of

this world that make it unique. Once, I was hiking down a mountain on the island of Crete, Greece when I met some _____

(man) who were shepherds. They were accompanied by _____ (dog) of various breeds that helped them guard and guide all

their _____ (sheep). They invited me to their village where they introduced me to their _____ (family) that included

not only their _____ (wife) and _____ (offspring) but also their _____ (parent) and other _____

(relative). Their _____ (child) further introduced me to the family's _____ (pet) such as _____ (goose),

_____ (chicken), and _____ (ox), as well as their _____ (pest) such as _____ (mouse). Although our

communication was limited because of language _____ (issue), we were able to understand each other by using our

_____ (body) as _____ (medium) for sign language. This experience was very entertaining and changed our

_____ (life). It is, after all, these simple _____ (phenomenon) of culture and society that are worth studying. They

become the _____ (basis) for our better understanding of the world. Just like _____ (photo), these real-life

_____ (snapshot) change our _____ (criterion) for evaluating our human environment.

Identifying Count (C) / Non-Count Nouns (NC)

A. Categorize each noun in **bold** according to its type (count/non-count) in the table that follows.

B. If the noun is count, then write its other number (singular or plural) in parentheses.

Archaeology (1) is a unique **study** (2), for it has no **beginning** (3) and no end. It is infinite as well as multi-faceted. On the one hand, it requires many hours of **studying** (4) in a **library** (5) while at the same time it mandates **research** (6) outside a confined **space** (7). Archaeologists have to work both with their hands and with their **intellect** (8) in order to uncover the **mysteries** (9) of **antiquity** (10) and provide us with their **interpretation** (11). They have to delve in ancient **manuscripts** (12), as well as meticulously dig the **earth** (13) for even the slightest **trace** (14) of **history** (15). In **defiance** (16) of any **obstacle** (17) that may stand in their **way** (18), **sand** (19), **mud** (20), or uncooperative **weather** (21), they must use their **education** (22), **equipment** (23), and **imagination** (24) to help us reconstruct the **past** (25), understand the present, and re-imagine the future.

Noun			
1. *archaeology* (NC)	8. _____	16. _____	24. _____
	9. _____	17. _____	25. _____
2. *study (C) (studies)*	10. _____	18. _____	
	11. _____	19. _____	
3. _____	12. _____	20. _____	
4. _____	13. _____	21. _____	
5. _____	14. _____	22. _____	
6. _____	15. _____	23. _____	
7. _____			

Using Count/Non-Count Nouns

A. Complete each sentence with the appropriate noun from the list below. Use each noun only once.

B. Add –s or –es to nouns if they should be in the plural.

adventure	boredom	enjoyment	height	information	luggage	patience	reading	traffic	travel
airport	coffee	flights	foundation	literature	make-up	powder	tea	time	weight
									wine

1. Air _**travel**_ can be a great _**adventure**_, so you have to be prepared for it.

2. Make sure you know all the important _____ before you leave for the _____.

3. Your _____ should be of the right _____, width, and _____.

4. You cannot carry any _____ or other liquids in the cabin.

5. You should also have no cosmetics with you such as _____, which includes things like _____, lotion, or _____.

6. To avoid the airport _____, you should try to check in as early as possible.

7. To avoid _____, bring some _____ with you because _____ can always be pleasant.

8. _____ between _____ may seem endless, so _____ is of great importance.

9. _____ or _____ can also help keep you awake and energetic.

10. Oh, and, of course, do not forget the _____ that lies ahead.

Identifying Linking / Intransitive / Transitive Verbs

A. Identify all the verbs in the passage below by underlining them.

B. Categorize each verb in the table that follows according to its type (linking/intransitive/transitive). Since all linking verbs are intransitive, include them only in the linking-verb column.

C. Next to each transitive verb, write its object in parentheses.

D. Next to each linking verb, write its subject complement in parentheses.

Today is a perfect day for a walk in the narrow streets of Venice, Italy. I wake up in a good mood, and everything feels right. The maze of paths, alleys, and dead-end streets does not frighten me. Though I have no map, I gradually become more familiar with this labyrinth. It seems very difficult to find my way, but I still find the whole process very amusing. Slightly disoriented, I allow myself to get lost. In my quest, I seek all things new; I touch the walls of hundreds of years, and I feel their strength; I smell the humidity of the air trapped in the alleys, and I hear the incomprehensible sounds of singing Italian. I sit down for a minute, close my eyes, and breathe. I open my eyes again; everything remains still and smells ancient, sounds melodic, looks inviting. I am not dreaming.

LINKING	TRANSITIVE	INTRANSITIVE
		wake up

Identifying Verb Forms

Ch 1 | Verbs | Forms

A. Categorize each verb form in **bold** according to its type in the table that follows.

B. Then complete the table with the rest of the forms of each verb.

C. Keep in mind that some of the verbs may be irregular, so you need to look up their forms in Chapter 2: Irregular Verbs Chart.

The real traveler **enjoys** (1) discovering remote and unknown sites. I always **pursue** (2) such opportunities, so the other day I **had** (3) a really unique experience in my effort to reach a small but demanding location. **Built** (4) on a hill with a view to the sea, this tiny church of Prophet Elijah **required** (5) a strenuous hike. The trail **was** (6) very difficult **to navigate** (7) as I tried **to battle** (8) the ferocious winds. However, at the end of the hike the **amazing** (9) view **rewarded** (10) my efforts.

Base Form	Simple Present (-s) form	Simple Past Tense (-ed) Form	Past Participle (-ed) Form	Present Participle (-ing) Form	Infinitive (to-) Form
enjoy	*enjoys*	*enjoyed*	*enjoyed*	*enjoying*	*to enjoy*
1.					
2.					
3.					
4.					
5.					
6.					
7.					
8.					
9.					
10.					

Identifying Descriptive Adverbs

A. Identify all descriptive adverbs in the sentences below by underlining them.

B. Write each adverb in the column to the right together with the word(s) it modifies. Put those words in parentheses.

C. Categorize each adverb according to what information it provides. Some may appear in more than one category.

1. Airports are underlined{absolutely} amazing places.

2. They are always full of life.

3. What I really enjoy about airports is people.

4. One can easily find very different nuances of human emotion at an airport: joy, grief, stress, panic.

5. Welcoming embraces, painful goodbyes, and erratic sprints are definitely part of any airport scene.

6. Lately airports have been mostly dominated by panic and fear of terrorism.

7. This is something travelers have to deal with locally and globally.

8. Unfortunately, we need to view this phenomenon as part of reality.

9. We should try to arrive early and proceed patiently.

10. We should never allow our fears to spoil our excitement for air-travel.

MANNER How?	PLACE Where?	TIME When?	DEGREE OF INTENSITY To What Degree?	QUANTITY How Much?	FREQUENCY How Often?
			absolutely	absolutely (amazing)	

Ch 1 | Adverbs | Types   Identifying Descriptive and Conjunctive Adverbs

A. <u>Underline</u> all adverbs in the following paragraph.
B. Categorize each adverb according to its type in the table that follows.

I will <u>never</u> forget my first visit to San Francisco. Everything felt utterly new and exciting. Indeed, it felt like the whole city belonged to me. I only had three days, yet I wanted to see everything. Therefore, I had to choose wisely. First, I decided I could not see everything. Hence, I immediately threw away my guidebook but kept my map; otherwise, I would be constantly lost. Furthermore, I wore my most comfortable shoes, and, finally, I braced myself with curiosity and excitement. It turned out that those four things were all I needed to fully enjoy the city.

DESCRIPTIVE
(Help Modify)

CONJUCTIVE
(Help Transition)

never

Distinguishing Between Adverbs and Adjectives

A. Categorize each of the words in **bold** as adjectives or adverbs.

B. Write the word(s) each adjective or adverb modifies next to it in parentheses.

C. Categorize each adverb according to what information it provides. Some may appear in more than one category.

SENTENCE	ADJECTIVE	ADVERB
1. The **daily** life of people in a **foreign** place can be **rather** interesting.	*foreign (place)*	
2. **Many** people watch the travel channel **daily**.		
3. **Greek** people are **mostly** known for their hospitality.		
4. I **recently** bought this **lovely** painting from a gallery in France.		
5. Even if you travel by yourself, you will **never** feel **lonely** in New York.		

MANNER	PLACE	TIME	DEGREE OF INTENSITY	QUANTITY	FREQUENCY
How?	Where?	When?	To What Degree?	How Much?	How Often?

Identifying Conjunction Types

A. Identify all conjunctions in the sentences below by <u>underlining</u> them.

B. Write each conjunction in the column to the right.

C. Identify each conjunction as coordinating (C), subordinating (S), or correlative (CR).

1. <u>When</u> people base their judgment of others on stereotypes, they fall prey to oversimplified beliefs.

   when (S) _____

2. This is a very common mistake because stereotypes are widespread in most cultures.

   _____

3. People tend to form stereotypes, for they don't see the underlying faulty reasoning.

   _____

4. If A, who is from country B, is obnoxious, then everyone from country B is obnoxious.

   _____

5. Therefore, not only do people over-expand their conclusions to everyone, but they also do not question these assumptions.

   _____

6. Whether it is the demanding American, the camera-obsessed Japanese, or the lazy Greek, stereotypes usually prejudice people against others.

   _____

7. It is important that we both recognize and avoid stereotypes.

   _____

8. Even though we may think of our evidence as sufficient, it is best to refrain from over-generalizing our conclusions.

   _____

9. We need to approach people's behavior with an open mind, so we understand them better.

   _____

10. Stereotypes promote neither mutual understanding nor collaboration among people.

   _____

Identifying Prepositions

A. Categorize each preposition (prepositional phrase) in **bold** according to its type/function as Adjective or Adverb.

B. Write the word(s) each preposition modifies next to it in parentheses.

Las Vegas offers visitors amazing opportunities **for entertainment** (1). **In addition to** (2) the traditional casino fun, Las Vegas also provides an environment designed **for family** (3). Indeed, most hotels advertise themselves **as family-friendly** (4) and feature water parks, roller coasters, and gigantic playgrounds. It is not rare that visitors will hardly spend any time **at the casinos** (5); **instead of** (6) trying their luck, many choose to experiment **with the plethora** (7) **of gourmet restaurants** (8), to wander **inside impressive hotels** (9), or to enjoy an extravagant show. The city has something **for every taste** (10).

Preposition as Adjective Modifies nouns and pronouns	Preposition as Adverb Modifies verbs, adverbs, adjectives, clauses
1. *(opportunities) for entertainment*	
2.	
3.	
4.	
5.	

Preposition as Adjective Modifies nouns and pronouns	Preposition as Adverb Modifies verbs, adverbs, adjectives, clauses
6.	
7.	
8.	
9.	
10.	

Appendix Chapter 2: Verb Tenses

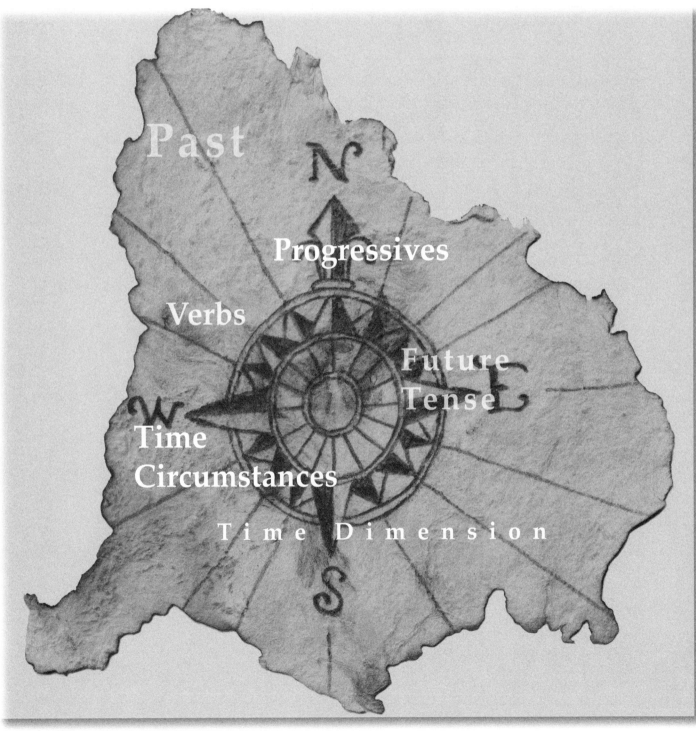

Using Present Tenses

A. Choose the correct present verb tense in the parentheses by underlining it. Keep in mind that not all options are in present tenses.

B. Identify the particular tense of each verb you chose in the right column.

Simple Present

_____

_____

_____

_____

_____

1. Architecture (<u>entails</u>, is entailing) the design of buildings and structures.

2. Mark currently (is studying, studied) to become an architect at the University of Chicago.

3. He always (had been, has been) interested in transforming the environment through buildings.

4. Since his first year in college, he (has been focusing, focuses) on Architecture as well as Art History.

5. He constantly (dreams of, is dreaming of) creating a great structure and through it gaining immortality.

6. Famous architects like Antoni Gaudi of Spain and the American, Frank Lloyd Wright, (are becoming, have become) an inspiration to Mark.

7. To further understand these famous creators, he (travels, is traveling) regularly to explore new places.

8. We actually (are watching, have been watching) him right now in a video from Barcelona, Spain.

9. He (is standing, has stood) in awe outside Gaudi's famous Roman Catholic Church, "La Sagrada Familia."

10. Construction of this church (has been taking place, has taken place) since 1882. Impressive!!

Forming Present Verb Tenses

A. Complete the table below with the forms of each verb. Try to retain the same person and number, and keep in mind that some of the verbs may be irregular.

B. In the space provided below, write a short paragraph about an architectural site that interests you. Try to use all the verbs from the table, but only in present tenses (you can use the verbs in a different person or number.)

Simple Present	Present Progressive	Present Perfect	Present Perfect Progressive
1. *it stands*			
2.		*I have admired*	
3.	*I am reading*		
4.			*I have been working*
5. *he shows*			

Using Past Tenses

A. Choose the correct past verb tense in the parentheses by underlining it. Keep in mind that not all verbs are in past tenses.

B. Identify the particular tense of each verb you chose in the right column.

Simple Past _____ _____ _____ _____ _____

1. Antoni Gaudi (was being, <u>was</u>) a Modernist architect, famous for his highly idiosyncratic style.

2. He (has lived, had lived, lived) and created his art in Spain between 1852 and 1926.

3. While he (grew up, was growing up), Gaudi always (had observed, was observing) nature and its elements.

4. As an architect, he (incorporated, had been incorporating) these natural elements in his work.

5. Although he (had not been earning, has not been earning) excellent grades in college, he already (was known, was being known, has been known) for his idiosyncratic style.

6. His devotion to Catholicism, which (had started, was starting) at an early age, (inspired, has inspired) him in his major project, "La Sagrada Familia" or "Sacred Family."

7. He constantly (had been working, is working) on it when an accident (occurred, was occurring) on June 7th, 1926.

8. As he (was walking, had been walking), he (is run over, was run over) by a tram and died three days after.

9. By the time of his death in 1926, he (had not yet completed, has not yet completed) "La Sagrada Familia."

10. As a tribute to his genius, the people of Spain (buried, had buried, were burying) Gaudi in the midst of his unfinished masterpiece.

Forming Past Verb Tenses

A. Complete the table below with the forms of each verb. Try to retain the same person and number, and keep in mind that some of the verbs may be irregular.

B. In the space provided below, write a short paragraph about an architectural site you have visited. Try to use all the verbs from the table, but only in past tenses (you can use the verbs in a different person or number.)

	Simple Past	Past Progressive	Past Perfect	Past Perfect Progressive
1.	she observed			
2.		I was driving		
3.			I had traveled	
4.		we were taking		
5.				you had been studying

Using Future Tenses

A. Choose the correct future verb tense in the parentheses by underlining it. Keep in mind that not all verbs are in past tenses.

B. Identify the particular tense of each verb you chose in the right column.

	Simple Future

1. When completed, Burj Dubai, or Dubai Tower, (<u>will be</u>, is) the tallest man-made building on Earth.

2. Keeping it a secret, the building companies (will reveal, will have revealed) the final height in September 2009.

3. Indeed, despite its current height at 2,087 ft, the tower's final height (will be announced, would be announced) only when its construction (will have been completed, was completed).

4. Based on current known facts, the Dubai Tower (will have, has) at least 164 floors by the end of construction.

5. It (will have broken, will have been breaking) the record for highest vertical concrete pumping at 1,972 ft.

6. Additionally, it (will have become, will be becoming) the tallest freestanding structure surpassing the CN Tower.

7. Until its completion, this tower (will have been continuously surpassing, is continuously surpassing) previous records for man-made structures.

8. However, it (will have also cost, had also cost) approximately 4.1 billion American dollars.

9. Standing among other impressive structures in Dubai Downtown, Burj Dubai (will be serving, will have been serving) as a testament to man's limitless ambition.

10. After September 2009, Burj Dubai (will be dwarfing, is dwarfing) any other structure on the globe, at least until the next ambitious endeavor.

Forming Future Verb Tenses

A. Complete the table below with the forms of each verb. Try to retain the same person and number, and keep in mind that some of the verbs may be irregular.

B. In the space provided below, write a short paragraph about an architectural site that you would like to see. Try to use all the verbs from the table, but only in future tenses (you can use the verbs in a different person or number.)

Simple Future	Future Progressive	Future Perfect	Future Perfect Progressive
1. *I will book*			
2.	*you will be taking*		
3.		*she will have stayed*	
4.			*he will have been spending*
5. *we will relax*			

Identifying All Verb Tenses

A. Identify all verbs in the sentences below by underlining them.

B. Identify the particular tense of each verb in the column to the right.

	Simple Past
1. June 2006 was my first time visiting New York City.	past perfect, simple past
2. I had heard, read, and seen so much about this city that my four-day trip was only a humble beginning.	past progressive, simple past
3. While the plane was approaching JFK airport, I kept revising my list of sight tours and things to do.	simple present
4. Four days, however, is just not enough for a city the size and magnitude of New York.	simple past
5. I took the train to Grand Central Station and found myself amidst the architectural maze of Manhattan.	past progressive, past progressive, simple present
6. As I was walking out to the busy streets of the metropolis, I was humming "I want to be a part of it! New York, New York!"	past perfect
7. By the end of my first day, I had only visited the Statue of Liberty, the World Trade Center monument, and the Empire State Building.	past perfect, past perfect, past progressive, simple present
8. I had also realized that I had run out of time.	present perfect, simple future
9. Two years later, I still think of those four days in NYC with great fondness and nostalgia.	
10. I have promised myself to go back, and I will keep my promise.	

Forming Irregular Verbs Correctly

Ch 2 | Verb Tenses | Irregular Verbs

A. Identify all verbs by underlining them.
B. Correct any errors in the form of irregular verb without changing the tense itself.

Since 1886 the Statue of Liberty, or Lady Liberty, has standed *stood* to welcome newcomers to the United States of America, the land

of opportunity. Originally conceived to commemorate the friendship and collaboration between France and the United States during

the American Revolution, the Statue of Liberty gradually becomed *became* a symbol of freedom, democracy, and friendship among nations. At

the time, the French side was responsible for the statue while the American side builded *built* the pedestal. When construction begun, *begun/begun*

sculptor Frederic Auguste Bartholdi was assigned with the design of the statue, but perhaps the biggest challenge that rose *arose* was funding

the projects on both sides of the ocean. Fortunately, many people maken *made* consistent efforts toward the completion of the project. In the

process of construction, for instance, the contribution of engineer Alexandre Gustave Eiffel—designer of the Eiffel Tower— was

proved *proven* a key person in solving structural problems; in the U.S., newspaper editor Joseph Pulitzer— noted for the Pulitzer Prize—

growed *grew* critical of American people for their lack of interest in the project and, thus, managed to increase donations for the pedestal.

Eventually, Lady Liberty arrived in New York City in 1875; she had been broke *broken* into 350 pieces to fit in 214 crates. Ever since her

assembly, she has keeped *kept* holding her torch and showing the way to "[the] tired, [the] poor, [the] huddled masses, yearning to be free."

Editing for Verb Tenses

Identify all verbs by underlining them **and** correct any verb tense errors.

Atop a hill of the Santa Monica mountains is sitting *sits* the Getty Center. Thanks to a generous founder, the J. Paul Getty Trust, an ingenious architect, Richard Meier, and a plethora of individuals, this architectural jewel was honoring the City of Los Angeles, California since 1997. Not only the museum collections, but also the privileged location of the site and its uniqueness in design and materials had made this center world-renowned. Indeed, the museum collections are constituting only a part of the tribute to Art that the Getty Center had been offering. Because the architect, Richard Meier, has been envisioning this project as a bridge between nature and culture, he designed it as an enormous window to nature. From atop, visitors daily have spent hours marveling at the view of the conjuring San Gabriel Mountains, the Pacific Ocean, and the city's ever-expanding street-grid. To further enhance natural light, Meier will be utilizing specific materials, the most fascinating of which was travertine. This beige, textured stone all will come from Bagni di Tivoli, Italy. For a year, while workers have extracted all 16,000 tons of travertine from the Italian quarries, Meier and his staff are developing a technique to retain the many fossils in the stone. Apparently, Meier thinks of using those as part of another art collection, ingrained in building materials. Last but not least in this amazing site is coming the 134,000-square-foot garden, designed by Robert Irwin as another contribution to Art. Undoubtedly, the Getty Center will have left any guest in awe of nature and the human spirit.

Editing for Verb Tenses

Identify all verbs by underlining them **and** correct any verb tense errors.

Frank Lloyd Wright <s>was</s> *is* still <u>regarded</u> as the most influential American architect. He has been born in 1867 in Richland Center, Wisconsin. Early in his childhood, his mother gives him a set of Froebel toys, which consisted of wood blocks and paper for construction. According to Wright, these toys have greatly influenced him in wanting to design rather than just draw. As a young adult, Wright was leaving for Chicago although he had been already attending two semesters of engineering, in the University of Wisconsin. In Chicago, he has been working for the architectural team of Adler and Sullivan for ten years, until he decided to freelance on his own. Another great influence on both his work and personal philosophy were being Japanese art and culture. One of the structures that Wright will be mostly famous for is the Kaufmann family House, known as Fallingwater. Since its construction in Western Pennsylvania in 1935, this house had been fascinating audiences. On top of a waterfall, Fallingwater is giving the impression of floating on water. No wonder, it has become instantly famous for its peculiar design and is being featured on Time magazine's cover in 1938. Today Fallingwater is a National Historic Landmark. Frank Lloyd Wright has been active and prolific through the end of his days in 1959. New York City's celebrated Guggenheim Museum was his swan song, for he dies during its construction.

Subject/Verb Agreement
General Principles

A. In the sentences below identify all the verbs by underlining them.

B. Identify the subject of each verb by circling it (here, in bold) and by crossing out any other elements of the subject (modifiers, adjectives, etc.).

C. Make sure each verb agrees with its subject in terms of number, person, and gender by making any necessary changes.

1. As an educational and research institution, the **University** of California has a very strong reputation.

2. There exist general consensus among scientists today in regards to the phenomenon of climate change.

3. In the past few years, there has been many people switching from an SUV to a hybrid car to lessen their carbon footprint.

4. Not only the individual but also companies needs to make an effort to become green in order to protect the environment.

5. Carbon dioxide and methane, two of the major greenhouse gases, helps to retain heat in the earth's atmosphere.

6. The consequences of the climate change phenomenon affects the whole planet and not only certain countries.

7. According to many scientists, renewable energy along with technological advances are the solution to this problem.

8. Political and business decisions play an important role in handling the phenomenon of climate change.

9. Fossil fuels and their products is one of the major contributors to climate change.

10. Collaboration and responsibility between people and their government constitutes a path to facing the challenge of climate change.

Subject/Verb Agreement

Nouns as Subjects

A. In the sentences below identify all verbs by underlining them.
B. Identify the subject of each verb by circling it (here, in bold) and by crossing out any other elements of the subject (modifiers, adjectives, etc.).
C. Make sure each verb agrees with its subject in terms of number, person, and gender by making any necessary changes.

1.   Usually my **students** are more technologically savvy than me.

2.   In most university classrooms chalk has been replaced with markers for dry-erase boards.

3.   Summer rain always come as a pleasant surprise to rejuvenate the dry soil and thirsty plants.

4.   Thanks to the Internet, informations has become easily accessible by millions of people.

5.   Unlike jogging, swimming do not strain nor harm a person' joints.

6.   Despite its importance in shaping the world, politics are unappealing to many young people.

7.   This activist group tries to protect many endangered species such as the polar bear.

8.   Although primarily American, the band hail from five different states.

9.   In the United States, four dollars seem like an exorbitant price for a gallon of oil.

10. Directed by Clint Eastwood, *Letters from Iwo Jima* were nominated for Best Picture in 2006.

Subject/Verb Agreement

Pronouns as Subjects

A. In the sentences below underline only the verbs that have a pronoun as a subject.

B. Identify the pronoun-subject of these verbs by circling it and by crossing out any other elements of the subject.

C. Make sure each of these verbs agrees with its subject in terms of number, person, and gender by making any necessary changes.

1. Instructors cannot help students **who** do not want to be helped.

2. As the mayor, I would like to thank all the volunteers who has helped replant the burnt forest.

3. This engagement ring is an heirloom which have been in my family for more than seven generations.

4. Celebrities are extravagant when, for instance, they buy jeans that costs three hundred dollars a pair.

5. Although everyone in these games have worked very hard, only one contestant can win the gold medal.

6. Every time Kevin returns from a trip abroad, nothing seems the same to him thanks to his new perspective.

7. Each among my students have a different way of learning and absorbing grammar.

8. Unfortunately, only few of my high-school friends have stayed in contact after the end of their senior year.

9. All of the parents attending the graduation ceremony was deeply moved and highly proud of their offspring.

10. People are often unaware that not all of the information found on websites come from valid sources.

Making Sure Verbs Agree With Their Subjects

Correct any Subject/Verb Agreement errors in the paragraph below (do not change the verb tenses). Try to find verbs and subjects first.

Among the most famous of ancient Greek tragedies are *Oedipus Rex* or *Oedipus the King*. Composed by Sophocles and first performed in 429 B.C., this tragedy is the first of a trilogy sequence, which consist of *Oedipus the King, Oedipus at Colonus,* and *Antigone.* According to many critics, there is very few tragedies comparable to this one. *Oedipus the King* is the story of Oedipus, son of Laius and Iocasta, king and queen of Thebes. Warned by an oracle that he will perish by the hand of his own offspring, Laius binds the feet of baby Oedipus with a pin and give him to a servant with the order to assassinate the infant. The servant, filled with pity, prove incapable of the brutal murder, so he abandons the baby in the mountains. A shepherd, who finds the baby, give him the name "Oedipus," which mean "swollen foot." Due to the shepherd's lack of means, the boy ends up being adopted by Polybus, King of Corinth, and his wife, Merope. In Corinth rumors and stories about Oedipus not being Polybus' biological son reaches Oedipus himself. Determined to discover the truth, he asks for the Delphi Oracle's help, but all he finds out is that he is doomed to sleep with his mother and kill his father. The news delivered by the Oracle are very disturbing, so Oedipus decides to leave Corinth in hopes to avert his destiny. Alas, all of this process only bring him closer to it, for neither his efforts nor his intellect are powerful enough to change it.

Making Sure Verbs Agree With Their Subjects

Correct any Subject/Verb Agreement errors in the paragraph below (do not change the verb tenses). Try to find verbs and subjects first.

Besides Oedipus the King, there is two more tragedies in Sophocles' famous trilogy; *Antigone* constitutes one of them. *Antigone* narrates the story of Oedipus' daughter in her quest for a legal system of morality. The action of the protagonists take place in Thebes following Oedipus' realization that he have killed his father and slept with his mother, Iocasta. After Oedipus voluntarily abandons his kingdom and go into exile, his sons, Eteocles and Polyneices, has a quarrel over ruling rights. Polyneices forms an alliance with the king of another city, Argos, and march against Thebes. However, his failed assault against Thebes are sealed by the two brothers who kills each other in battle. The day after the fatal battle, Creon, now king, issue a decree which declares Polyneices a traitor and prohibit anyone from honoring him with a proper burial. These orders is what Antigone but also her fiancé and son of Creon, Aemon, and the wife of Creon, decides to challenge, for they opposes divine law. As a consequence not only Antigone but also her fiancé and son of Creon, Aemon, and the wife of Creon, Eurydice, perishes. Antigone is executed for her disobedience while Aemon and Eurydice commit suicide. In her struggle, Antigone declares her defiance toward human law that is not in harmony with divine law. For this, many has considered Antigone to be an emblem of justified civil disobedience. Although approximately twenty-five-hundred years have passed since *Antigone* was written, she still symbolizes the struggle of free-thinking individuals against tyrannical and totalitarian regimes.

Pronoun/Antecedent Agreement
General Principles

A. In the sentences below identify all pronouns (that have an antecedent) by underlining them.

B. Identify the antecedent of each pronoun by circling it (here, in bold).

C. Make sure each pronoun agrees with its antecedent in terms of number, person, and gender by making any necessary changes.

1. **My family and I** enjoy spending quality time together, so we often attend shows or go on trips together.

2. As the youngest in the family, Jim did not only have everyone's guidance, but she also had to meet everyone's expectations.

3. Considering a pet as part of the family, many people name it after humans, celebrate it's birthday, and dress them up.

4. A doctor has to go through years of rigorous training, and personal sacrifices to earn his degree.

5. The CEO of a company is the person who usually signs his name on most official documents regarding the company.

6. An experienced nurse can give you her opinion on the side-effects of most drugs.

7. Students, instructors, and administrators gathered together to support their school's debate team at the national contest.

8. The leading actress in the movie was alarmed when she discovered in his purse a cell phone that was not her.

9. Not only the parents but also the brave firefighter, Jason, put their life at risk to rescue the baby in the flooded apartment.

10. Neither the prosecutor nor the defendants were able to prove their case to the jury and the judge.

Pronoun/Antecedent Agreement

Nouns as Antecedents

A. In the sentences below identify all pronouns (that have an antecedent) by underlining them.

B. Identify the antecedent of each pronoun by circling it (here, in bold).

C. Make sure each pronoun agrees with its antecedent in terms of number, person, and gender by making any necessary changes.

1. **English** is notorious for its numerous **idioms** and **expressions** which always confuse non-native speakers.

2. Learning about water and his importance as well as scarcity may help people think twice before taking a long shower.

3. Not only did the assigned homeworks help me understand the concept, but they also helped me ace the final.

4. Jane's hair is very thick and lush, but it shows signs of damage because of all the heavy processing.

5. The detective found two hairs at the crime scene, and it may help with the investigation of the murder.

6. In order to understand statistics, a person has to study their principles and appreciate it's value.

7. Memorization can sometimes be an effective learning strategy if it is accompanied by critical thinking.

8. The class casted their votes in favor of high standards and objective grading.

9. The government informed his members of a new strategy to manage the national deficit.

10. The Board of Directors announced their unanimous decision to raise membership fees.

Ch 4 | Agreement |
Pronoun/Antecedent

Pronoun/Antecedent Agreement

Pronouns as Antecedents

A. In the sentences below identify all pronouns (that have an antecedent) by underlining them.

B. Identify the antecedent of each pronoun by circling it (here, in bold).

C. Make sure each pronoun agrees with its antecedent in terms of number, person, and gender by making any necessary changes.

1. **Anyone** can construct ~~his~~ *his/her* personal page on Facebook or MySpace and can share information with friends.

2. Both agreed on a two-month truce to re-establish diplomatic relationships and negotiations between them.

3. According to the Chinese concept of yin and yang, everything has their opposing but complementary aspects.

4. All of the defendants had to submit his/her passports before being released on bail.

5. All of this food was produced locally, so it is very fresh and fragrant.

6. At the end of each year, one has to look in the mirror and be honest with himself/herself.

7. My hope as an instructor is that each of my students will reach their potential.

8. The Declaration of Independence ensures that nobody is deprived of his inalienable rights.

9. Much of this explanation is redundant, for it keeps repeating the same things over and over again.

10. Several among the audience were willing to share his stories in public, something that was very courageous.

Exercise #9

Pronoun/Antecedent Agreement

Avoiding Sexist Language

Rewrite the following sentences in a way that avoids sexist language but does not change the meaning of the sentence.

1. Any politician has to try his best to overcome the stereotype that all politicians are liars.

   • _____

2. An avid video-gamer spends much of his time at the computer playing or chatting about the game with other gamers.

   • _____

3. Every competent kindergarten teacher can keep her students busy with interesting and constructive games.

   • _____

4. In a democracy a citizen not only can voice his opinion freely, but he should also try to do so.

   • _____

5. For any operation to be successful, the surgeon relies on his team to be quite knowledgeable, competent, and responsive.

   • _____

Making Sure Pronouns Agree With Their Antecedents

In the paragraph below underline all pronouns and correct any Pronoun/Antecedent Agreement errors.

After Annie graduated from college, he found oneself at a crossroads.

During one's college years, many people had been puzzled by her major, for one could not understand what it means to be a

philosopher. Annie would try to explain that a philosopher is a person who uses her critical thinking skills to analyze issues such as life

and their purpose, death, morality. Herself would also mention names of famous philosophers such as Socrates, Aristotle, Kant,

Rousseau, yet it was only met with more puzzlement. The usual follow-up questions to Annie's explanation would be "What kind of

position can you get as a philosopher?" or "How much money can he make in philosophy?" Some would even question society's need

for such a profession, and he/she would mock Annie for being a "loser." Gradually, Annie grew tired of his questions, ignorance, and

focus on money, so he stopped trying to explain anything to us. With the degree in its hand, however, she still needed to think about

job applications or possibly graduate school. Society today seems focused on more pragmatic aspects of life, so he mostly values those

members whose can put a price tag on his work-output. Clearly, this decision was going to be a great challenge for Annie. However, it

would be hers philosophical background and training in analysis that would assist him with choosing the right professional path.

- **Sentence Correction:** _____

5. Being very indecisive about choosing a major.
   - **Sentence Error ID:** _____
   - **Sentence Correction:** _____

6. In this grammar handbook includes thorough explanations and multiple examples of sentence errors.
   - **Sentence Error ID:** _____
   - **Sentence Correction:** _____

7. Before being exposed to different cultures through traveling, books were Paul's main source of information about the world.
   - **Sentence Error ID:** _____
   - **Sentence Correction:** _____

8. Keith has been for the English Department working as a lecturer for the last seven years.
   - **Sentence Error ID:** _____
   - **Sentence Correction:** _____

9. Kate, after her one-year tour of Europe, has gained a different perspective on many issues.
   - **Sentence Error ID:** _____
   - **Sentence Correction:** _____

10. When Adela was an exchange student abroad) (helped her practice her Spanish and meet people from other countries.
    - **Sentence Error ID:** _____
    - **Sentence Correction:** _____

Correcting Sentence Errors

In the paragraph below, find and correct any sentence errors (fragments, run-ons, comma splices, misplaced and dangling modifiers). Remember that the safest way to edit for sentence errors is to isolate your sentences and clauses, so it may be better to start by completing Exercise #8. Keep in mind that more than one ways of correction may be appropriate.

Dear Students,

There comes in our lives–a time in our lives. When we all have to look at ourselves in the mirror. Usually mirrors do not lie, but we choose not to see the truth about ourselves. Indeed, many times we try to take credit only for our successes; while we refuse to take responsibility for our failures. Instead, we often try to blame our failures on others, we tend to complain about our bad luck. Blaming instructors for harsh grades, laziness is what instructors blame students for. If we closely and honestly look, however, the mirror will be honest too it will reveal both our strengths and our weaknesses. When we analyze the causes of our successes or failures can be the source of invaluable lessons. Following this strategy, future problems will not be too challenging because we will be ready to overcome them. If we take a brave look in the mirror will tell us the truth.

Identifying Sentence Errors

A. In the column to the left, write out the sentences from Exercise #7.
B. For each sentence, identify any existing errors by underlining them and writing their ID in the column to the right. If the sentence is correct, write CORRECT.

Misplaced Modifier

1.   There comes <u>in our lives</u> a time.

2.

3.

4.

5.

6.

7.

8.

9.

10.

Correcting Sentence Errors

In the paragraph below, find and correct any sentence errors (fragments, run-ons, comma splices, misplaced and dangling modifiers). Remember that the safest way to edit for sentence errors is to isolate your sentences and clauses, so it may be better to start by completing Exercise #10. Keep in mind that more than one ways of correction may be appropriate.

PHILOSOPHY & PLATO

Philosophy derives from the Greek words "philo" and "sophia"; *which mean* "love" and "wisdom" accordingly. This love for knowledge urges people to seek answers to questions regarding abstract matters ; such as life, reason, and truth. One of the most famous Greek philosophers was Plato his "Allegory of the Cave" is still taught at universities all over the world. Because he investigates the nature of truth and reality in this piece makes this allegory a classic one. By using the metaphor of a man trying to escape from a cave, the effort of this man shows humans' struggle to discover truth. Plato is famous for also his account of the teachings of Socrates. Furthermore, to be truly informed on his work, Plato's epic work, *The Republic*, must be studied. In this book describes an idealistic, utopian world, governed by citizens. In many ways *The Republic* has served as a model for the government systems of the Roman Empire and of the modern United States of America therefore we can observe continuity in the teachings of philosophers from the past to the present.

Identifying Sentence Errors

A. In the column to the left, write out the sentences from Exercise #9.

B. For each sentence, identify any existing errors by underlining them and writing their ID in the column to the right. If the sentence is correct, write CORRECT

Correct

1. Philosophy derives from the Greek words "philo" and "sophia";

2.

3.

4.

5.

6.

7.

8.

9.

10.